Still Spinning!

Barbara J. Henderson

PAGE PUBLISHING, INC.
Conneaut Lake, PA

First originally published by Page Publishing 2019

ISBN 978-1-64424-708-2 (pbk)
ISBN 978-1-64424-709-9 (digital)

Printed in the United States of America

Acknowledgement

To my family and friends to numerous to name individually, you know who are. Love to you for caring enough to encourage and not discourage. Thanks is not enough!

Patricia Hightower (my sister, my rock), my friend Bonnie Sugarman retired VP APA Talent agency, my nephew William 'Billy' Hobbs PHD, faithful friend, novelist Quyntin Newberne nudged me on when I neeed nudging most. They gave new meaning to the word nudge. Thank You!!!

In 1948, all a colored young girl in Detroit could ask for was hopscotch, a red Schwinn bike with the bell, and Monopoly on a rainy day with my family. Romantic love was not in the picture, or so I thought. William "Billy" Henderson and I met when we were ten and eleven years of age. He was light-brown-skinned, handsome, and husky in stature, with a smile that made you believe you could float on air. I wasn't so bad-looking myself, mind you. I, too, was fair-skinned and sported the kind of mole just over my lip that folks used to draw on their faces with mascara pens. Yes, at that age, attraction is all you can call it. In time, it was that and so much more.

Billy and I went to the George Washington Carver Elementary School in Royal Oak Township. Carver school was not the biggest. You went from kindergarten to the eighth grade, so it was like one big family. The school is in Royal Oak Township, which is in Ferndale, Michigan, a suburb of Detroit. Royal Oak Township begins at 8 Mile Road, which is the baseline of Detroit (eight miles from the Detroit City Hall) and ends at 9 Mile Road in Royal Oak. One side of 8 Mile was Ferndale, and the other side was Detroit. Michigan was named after one of the Great Lakes: Lake Erie, Lake Huron, Lake Michigan, and Lake Superior. The part that Detroit occupied was basically flat terrain. Michigan was surrounded by the Great Lakes.

We lived in government housing projects within the lake's flat terrain. The whole area was called the "mile." This is how you identified where you were from. It really didn't matter to anyone where you were from, as long as it was from either side. If you were from anywhere else, things could get dicey; locals were known to get into confrontations with so-called outsiders.

Such concerns were far from my mind in those days, when roller skating was the fun thing to do. Being kids with little to no money, we found "almost free" fun things to do. Skating definitely played its part as one of the favorites. Wouldn't you know, Billy and I kept running into each other at the Duke skating, rink which used to be the Duke movie theater. You should have seen him, with his tightly packed, low-cut hair. He offered to teach me how to skate backward. It just so happened that skating backward was the time to, as the young folks might say today, "get your cuddle on." There was a backward skating contest on this particular night. Billy talked me into entering the contest as his partner.

Wearing my black, cat-eye-framed glasses, I was frightened and too inexperienced at skating backward, but as "The Glory of Love" by the Five Keys began to play, we made our way into the flow of the skaters. I took a deep breath, checked the bow on my ponytail, and turned around. As a light breeze came across my neck, Billy lay a hand on the waist of my poodle skirt.

"Just relax. Lean on me. I've got you."

Well, I listened to him at some points, closing my eyes to cherish the moment, and test him. Would he keep others from my path? Could he keep me from falling? He did so much so that we won the contest. I cannot, for the life of me, remember what the prize was that night. All I knew was his hand at my waist told me more than I could articulate at such a young age and that he had won my trust that night at the Duke.

Billy used to call me his dream girl (Hah! That is, before I became his nightmare.) He would say later that he always had a crush on me, but he felt he didn't measure up to my standards. That didn't come as a surprise to me. I always thought there were marked differences between us, even though we both lived in the projects.

Life dealt my family a rough hand, but we were happy and had the silliest of times. We even had a pet or two. I remember one dog's name was Trouble, and he slept with my brother. One day we heard the dog yelping very loudly.

My mother asked, "What the heck is going on?"

My brother answered, "He (Trouble) bit me, so I bit him back."

That never happened again.

There were six children in my family (four girls, one boy, and one of my mother's brothers). My grandmother died, and her four boys were divided among family members rather than having the state take care of them. My uncle, Bobby, was around the same age as one of my sisters.

My father worked at Dodge Main Automobile Plant when he slipped on some oil and broke his leg. (There was no such thing as Workmen's Compensation in those days.) This was at the end of World War II. As a result of my father's accident, he was given time to recuperate with no paycheck.

A friend of my parents told my father not only about government housing, but that there was work available. My mother worked at the Hudson Motor Car Plant in the Riveting Department as a "Rosie the Riveter" for the war effort. She had to take three streetcars to and from work. My father decided it was too much for her and asked her to stay home with the five of us kids (six, including her brother).

My father got the job with the housing authorities as a maintenance man. We moved to the projects. It was quite an adjustment being in a house with strangers separated by a very thin wall (you could actually hear the conversation from the other side if you listened hard enough). But my dad did what he had to.

My father did what he had to in order for us not to get comfortable in that situation, but to strive for better. The housing was only supposed to last ten years. Well, needless to say, most people lived there for at least twenty years. I can't remember my father ever just working one job. He was like a jack-of-all-trades, and master of none. He cooked at a restaurant, sold eggs out of an egg truck, painted furniture stores, and whatever else he could find in addition to his main job.

While living in the government housing, I remember taking piano lessons in elementary school. My teacher was Mrs. Bertha Hansberry Phillips, the mother of Lorraine Hansberry, the author of the play *Raisin in the Sun*. She also gave my mother piano lessons when she was a child. She stayed in a really nice house near the projects. Her house was red brick with a front porch the width of the house. There was black, wrought-iron railing on the edge as an enclosure so that you could sit outside. Inside the front door leading to the front room was a staircase leading to the second floor. This is where our bedrooms were. There were three bedrooms upstairs with one large bathroom. The house reminded me of the house we moved from. I often spent the weekends with her and helped her around the house.

Due to the lessons, I was the class pianist for my graduation from elementary school. I later went to the Detroit Conservatory of Music. I took thirteen and one half years of classical piano. I wanted to study pop music, but that was discouraged by my teachers. All five of us, as children, took piano lessons. I was the only one to remain dedicated. Consequently, I developed an appreciation for all kinds of music, eventually even learning to write it. This was one of the things my father would speak of to others with a swelled chest.

My mother soon got a job, primarily as a food server at the local hospital. She used to crochet and taught me how. I enjoyed certain crafts I did with my hands. I also learned to knit, paint, sew, and decorate clothing with jewels, etc. In addition to the crafts, I really enjoyed reading, so much so that I found myself reading dictionaries, encyclopedias, and whatever was informative. English, Journalism, and History became my favorite subjects in school. Reading would take me outside of my surroundings to new places.

Billy's family was somewhat distant with each other, whereas my family was very close. We did a lot of things together, things many would write off as trivial, but they meant the world to us. We kids, for instance, would meet my father at his job and race him home. He worked within walking distance of where we lived. On days when the weather was too bad for us to play outside, we played Monopoly. This was special to us as children because my dad always made us goodies. He would make Rice-Krispy treats, bake cookies, or whatever he would think of. Because he was a restaurant cook, I thought of him as a chef. He always experimented with food and was quite good at it. He made up some great recipes. Bologna Foo Yung was one of them. Daddy made cooking more interesting than anything else related to housekeeping or household chores. He made the food pleasing to the senses in every way. He took the ingredients for Egg Foo Yung and replaced the meat with bologna, thus a cheaper version for us. It was as if we had a restaurant in our very own project.

Each week a list of chores was placed on the door of the pantry. Everybody had a different job. When it came to the dishes, we rotated on a weekly basis. I remember us asking for a dishwasher. My mother's reply was, "Why buy a dishwasher when I have six dishwashers?" She meant us, of course.

Friday was family court day. We always held court so everybody that had a grievance, or just something to say, could do so. That always seemed to amaze people. In a time where children were to be seen and not heard, we were taught to be independent and to think for ourselves. Everyone had a right to be heard.

I remember the time I went to see Mr. Hatcher, my father's boss. There were no recreational facilities for the families in the housing projects, so I went to see Mr. Hatcher with a few suggestions. He told my father he had an unexpected visit from Miss Barbara Ford, suggesting recreation for the children in the projects. Hatcher said that I had some pretty good ideas and proceeded to implement some of them. My dad asked my mother if she knew anything about it. She said no because I had not discussed the ideas with anyone else. I was thinking about the kids and what we needed. We soon had afterschool activities and recreation. These are some of the things that came from having our family court.

Mamma and Daddy were the judges, and we were the jury. We, the jury, decided on the punishment for whoever the defendant was. My dad and mother said to us years later that we were harder on ourselves than they would have been. Holding court was a fair way of dealing with complaints and keeping down arguments. One of the greatest memories about being a child was being able to freely talk with my parents even in my teen and adult years, and especially with my mother about anything. I just knew every family did the same things as mine. Boy, was I wrong.

Billy's mother had eight children to care for, and he never talked about her working or having the time or temperament for such activities. He told me about how his father had passed for white so that he could work at the post office. Billy said his father was fired when someone recognized him. He spoke about how handsome his family was on his father's side and how some of them passed for white. It wasn't as though his family did not try for better. Both families were present and hardworking. It's just that mine came into and was able to keep positions that had a higher status, and therefore, the family took on more middle-class sensibilities. I didn't know that there was status in the projects until I found out about Billy's situation. He knew it right away.

During this time of my life, I seldom saw Billy. We went our separate ways after elementary school. I started high school and grew up. I always loved acquiring knowledge, so school was relatively easy for me. I learned early on that if I stay on my studies, things would go a lot easier for me and consequently be more fun. My parents were strict about our whereabouts, so I stayed in activities that kept me after school. Honor Roll, Student Council, French Club, Cheerleader, Band, etc. were a few of the things that I stayed to attend. By the time I got home, the family usually had eaten, and the dishes and chores were done. My plate of dinner would always be in the oven.

My mother caught on to me and gave me an extra chore to do on Saturdays. I had a scrub board and had to handwash the family's socks. We had a sock bag; dirty socks were placed in it all week. The idea was to keep up with the mates to each sock. There were seven people who wore socks. This was an awfully smelly job. My brother's and my father's socks were so bad I had to change the wash water. I dreaded Saturdays, but after all, fair is fair. *One day was better than a week of washing dishes,* I thought.

After elementary school (remember, there was no such thing as middle school), we were supposed to go Ferndale High School. It was overcrowded, so we had to take buses to Northern High. In those days, that was the only way that was convenient to get to and from school. Every morning, six to eight buses would be at Carver Elementary School to take us to Northern. There was nothing political about busing then.

There was always a mad rush to catch the bus because if you missed it, you would have to take a city bus and then the streetcar and pay for it out of your pocket, or miss school and face your mother. The same applied if you missed the return trip. Busing was being paid for by either the school system or the US government, thereby making it free to the students who had to ride since we lived in government housing.

While I attended Northern High, I was in the same homeroom or study hall as Cecil Franklin, Aretha's brother, "Smokey" Robinson, and Bill Withers. Cecil followed his father's footsteps and became a minister. Smokey and Bill later became famous singers and songwriters.

While we were in school, one of the favorite pastimes was trying to harmonize and sing. I belonged to a girl's group named The Paraders. My sisters, Delores and Patricia, were in the group before I was; I was a stand-in. Meanwhile, Billy Henderson and Crathman Spencer started a group call the Domingos. (Later they would change their name to The Spinners after the spinner hubcaps on cars because there were several groups called the Domingos.) Both The Paraders and Spinners groups were actually good. The Paraders weren't as serious as The Spinners though. We dated and pursued other things.

High school, which came directly after elementary school, brought many changes. In came newfound independence and the changing of the way we wore our hair and clothes. I was fourteen when I started the ninth grade and officially beyond Wrangler jeans or dresses with puffed sleeves and belts that tied to the back. No more braids either. Now bobby socks, poodle skirts, and saddle oxfords were the standard. I learned all this from a good friend, Eugenia Ferguson, who gently informed me that I was now in high school and should dress differently. I told my parents, and they agreed.

Things went quite well from there. In fact, I remember that I loved school so much I excelled and won a full scholarship while in the ninth grade to Fisk University in Tennessee. My parents agreed with my counselor that I was too young to be attending college at that time. Needless to say, I stayed where I was, and that opportunity never came again because I didn't have the same drive to try for another scholarship.

I was in the school band as well as being a cheerleader. At that time, we had basketball and football games at night. When the band played, I didn't cheer for the games. There was this boy in the band named Charles Ross. He played first chair tenor saxophone. He and I started liking each other. Oh, Charles. He had a car and would take me home from a lot of the games. Pretty soon we were going steady with the permission of my dad and mom.

Charles joined the Air Force after graduation from school. He was my first real boyfriend, and we fell in love. When he went away, we really missed each other. My heart was set on going to college. We decided that if we got married after I graduated high school, I could still go to college. The University of Illinois was in Champaign, Illinois, about fifteen miles from Chanute Air Force Base, where Charles was stationed. We decided to get married. Our parents decided that if this was what we wanted, then they would help us. The wedding took place on the front lawn of my parent's home in the projects.

The day of the wedding I remember waking up and telling my mother I didn't want to get married. She said to me, "You're just nervous. Try to take a nap until it is time." It was too late to back out. All the money that was spent on the wedding gown and the reception would have been wasted, and we weren't rich by any means. I should have given the matter more thought. I was so naive I even took my roller skates on my honeymoon. At seventeen years old and having just graduated from high school, I had no clue what being a wife or possibly a mother entailed. It was as if I skated backward into adulthood with no one to guide me.

Well, after we were married, we moved to air base housing, and I still looked forward to getting into college. By the time the next semester came, however, I was pregnant. School had to be put on the back burner. I gave birth to a beautiful baby boy. We decided to name him after his father; only we would call him Chucky so we could distinguish between the two. Charles and I were happy for a while, and then fifteen months later, we had a second son. We named him Michael Clarence after Charles' father, Clarence.

Two children at such a young age overwhelmed the two of us. Tragically, Michael died of crib death or S.I.D.S. (sudden infant death syndrome) at the age of two months. His death somehow caused the slow deterioration, and destruction, of our marriage. Chucky was a big part of my maintaining my sanity during those trying times. For some reason, his father distanced himself from Chucky as well as me. I found myself being a single parent.

Charles was the air base general's driver and soon volunteered for overseas duty. He volunteered to go to Okinawa, Japan. He made arrangements for me and Chucky to go back to Detroit and live with his parents for a while.

After returning to Detroit, I found a job as a dental assistant for a young dentist right out of dental college. It was a very interesting career that just sort of fell into my lap. I wound up going to University of Detroit Dental College also. After I completed school, I was certified as a dental assistant and was taught to be a dental hygienist by Dr. Richard Snowden, for whom I worked. This job lasted twenty-six years on and off.

In the interim, I became a bookkeeper for the Detroit Board of Education. I worked as a troubleshooter bookkeeper for six years. This position took up my time in the day and evenings (night school). On the evenings I had off, I worked as a dental assistant/hygienist/office manager. Three jobs enough for three people. Although I was not in the best of situations, I wanted to live a certain way, and this is what it took. I enjoyed the positions, so it was not difficult. The most important factor in all of the decision-making, jobwise, was my son.

This phase of my life was challenging as well as exciting. I was on my own with a child and had no idea where I was heading and what I was to become when I would finally grow up, so to speak. I didn't understand anything about relationships. I always thought that you should be married if you were to have a lasting sexual kinship with someone.

Such a kinship was far from my mind at the time; I was determined to have a permanent, secure, comfortable home for me and my son. My son deserved the same upbringing and experiences I had coming up, so I moved into my first apartment, thus beginning a new life. In the meantime, my father's parents passed and left Daddy some money, which brought a dynamic into the family no one was ready for. He was an only child.

My mother and father had a home built on the Detroit side of 8 Mile Road. It was a beautiful house in a nice neighborhood. I remember that even though the five of us children were now adults with our own children (my uncle Bobby was in the army now), Mama and Daddy had us sign our names in the wet cement of the driveway next to the new house. This was a way of letting us know that we still had a place that was, collectively, our home. Everything was going along fine, we all thought. My father, being the only child, and having received this willed money, had other plans. He often at times told us as children that when we were grown, he was going to do some traveling, that he was going to leave. I never took him seriously. He did though.

Daddy and Mama were married for twenty-six years when the wanderlust hit Daddy hard. Mama worked at a hospital and tried to make a home for all concerned. We had another chance to be in our own house, out of the housing projects.

One day after fixing my mother breakfast in bed and emptying their joint bank account, Daddy packed some of his clothes and left. Daddy and Mama would marry three times in forty-seven years.

When Daddy left that first time, Mama never had a clue it was coming, and it devastated her and, also consequently, us children. I left my apartment and moved back home to help smooth the transition. For the first time, there was no man in the house. Mama filed for a divorce.

It just so happened that I was getting a divorce from Charles, and my baby sister (Pat) moved in with her daughter, Tangela, and was also getting a divorce. Mama and I continued to work, and Pat, who had dropped out of high school to get married and have her baby, went back and graduated with Cum Laude honors. We were quite proud of her determination to get her education in spite of all obstacles and did what we could to see that she experienced all that she missed out on. Her prom approached, and the money situation was tight for us. I had a beautiful green peau de soie silk gown that happened to fit Pat everywhere but in the bosom. We made it work; we stuffed her bosom with Kleenex tissue.

Pat said later that evening, while she was dancing with a guy, he mentioned that she was losing something. Pat stuffed the tissue back in and continued her evening of fun.

The neighbors became distant. Back in those days, divorce was not commonly accepted. The wives kept a close eye on their husbands. None of the wives allowed their husband to help us with anything.

It was a very awkward time for us. We found ourselves struggling, but relieved to a point. We did not have a man among us lording over everything. It was not long before everything became all right. By example of my mother, we became strong women. We survived those times and moved on to better days. It was good to be able to raise our children together. Times were not the best, nor were they the worst. All in all, being together made everything easier. Our support for each other proved stronger than we could have ever imagined. Every benefit has its cost, I suppose. People have their needs. It wasn't long before we started dating. Even Mama met someone.

My adventures in that area took a few unusual turns. I soon met a man named Henry Ford. I dated a man named John Beckley, and through him, I met Henry's sister, Dorothy, and her husband, Jerome.

The four of us decided to take a vacation together. We wound up in Waterloo, Iowa, which was Dorothy's home. Waterloo was the home of the packing house for Rath Bacon. The whole town reeked of slaughtered pork. It was the worst odor I ever smelled. We were to be there for two weeks. I got so sick from the smell it took my appetite. I wasn't the best company for anyone.

I wound up staying home a lot while I was there. Henry and his mother were very comforting to me while I was there. I began to lose weight because I couldn't eat.

Henry was about six feet tall with a medium complexion and very handsome with a so-called six-pack (it was more like a four-

and-a-half-pack, but I wasn't complaining.) Henry was also about five years younger than I. He had ambitions of becoming a baseball player. We became closer, while John and I became estranged. We were falling in love.

After the vacation, John and I broke up. Henry and I kept in touch. We decided after a short while that we should get married because we were "in love." I moved to Waterloo, Iowa, and we got married.

Henry and I decided that he would go ahead with his baseball plans. He applied to the minor league. He went to baseball camp but failed the training. He said he was distracted, that it wasn't an issue of his ability. He claimed he could not concentrate on baseball with me at home away from him. Being a traditional guy, he didn't want me to work. We then moved to Minneapolis, where employment was more available. He got a job in construction so that I wouldn't have to work. Being a stay-at-home wife was fine until I became bored, and he showed his jealousy and possessiveness. When we had company visiting, he picked me up, literally, and took me into another room when he thought it was time for them to leave. This happened no matter who it was, family or not. He was great with Chucky, but I couldn't stand to be smothered his way. That is when I realized that we were too far apart mentally! I didn't know what to look for in a marriage.

Before I realized it, I had been married four times. The last marriage (before Billy) was so traumatic I silently swore off getting married again for a while. My friends and family began calling me the Black Liz Taylor. I didn't like it, but if the shoe fits, what do you do? One of my mother's friends told me, "At least you got married and didn't shack up or live with them."

One day Billy and I ran into each other, and he invited me to see a show with The Spinners and Marvin Gaye at the Twenty Grand Lounge in Detroit. I wanted to see the show and the rest of the guys. We went to elementary school together, and I had not seen them for a long time.

The Spinners opened the show for Marvin. After he performed, Billy and I watched Marvin Gaye together. He was a close friend to Marvin. They used to play golf together.

We started seeing each other. We wanted to catch up on what we missed during the times we had not seen one another. Although he was very interested in my life, he couldn't understand my multiple marriages. I couldn't explain it to him because I didn't understand it myself. All I knew was that I felt a sense of both calm and excitement seeing him. By then, he had these sideburns going on that added another dimension to his face and his always perfect afro— you just don't understand.

Soon we dated. At that time, I worked as a bookkeeper and dental office manager in the evenings. Billy struggled with his career at Motown. He was sort of the man out front for the group. He took charge of his life, steering things along as he did with me in the skating rink.

In the meantime, I started to learn more about life for myself. Take racism, for instance. We were so naive about racism one day my sister Delores and I walked to downtown Detroit from high school. We walked in order to have some spending money. When we got to where we were going, we stopped in at a lunch count and ordered a hamburger and something to drink. The waitress kindly informed us that they reserved the right to serve whomever they wanted to and did we see the sign that was posted. The sign read, "We reserve the right to serve whomever we please." We both said yes and continued with our orders. The waitress shook her head and served us. When we got home, we asked my mother what the whole thing meant. My mother laughed at us and explained that we just experienced a form of racism.

That was my first experience. Another time, I was reading a story about a poor Negro family living in the south. I felt so sorry for them. I remember telling my mother and father that they should read about this poor Negro family. My father made the comment to my mother, "Do you suppose the girl doesn't know (she's colored and poor)?"

Billy and I talked about that and a lot of other subjects, things we never talked about with too many other people. We began to bond through our talks. I began to see that everybody didn't have the same freedom and advantages that I had as a child.

Billy told me that there were eight children in his family, and he was the oldest. He said a lot of responsibility was his as far as keeping an eye on his siblings. He said he spent many a hungry day because he never got enough to eat. He also said that he would have his shoes half-soled so often the shoe repairman told him that he need not bother trying to hold buying a new pair any longer. My heart went out to him for having to suffer through such times. He had been married and had two sons, Sterling and Joseph. He was now divorced.

Billy and I started officially dating in 1968. He had this adorable little paunch and sprouted to the height of five feet seven inches to my five feet. The Spinners, who sang with five-part harmony, had a hit record called "It's a Shame," written by Stevie Wonder and his then wife, Syreeta Wright. It was a big hit for them. We dated casually for a while because he was living with someone, and I wasn't interested in getting serious. He said he had to take care of the situation he was in because the girl was from out of town and didn't have anyone in Detroit. She was also someone he was grooming to sing professionally. (She would later become one of The Supremes.) This situation was perfect for me, I thought.

After about six months, things began to change for us. We became more involved. We started going horseback riding on weekends when Billy didn't have gigs. He owned a horse called Freddie and kept him stabled in Canada across the Detroit River.

David Ruffin, The Funkadelics, one of the Marvelettes, "Shorty" Long ("Here Comes the Judge"), and quite a few more recording artists all had horses at the same stables. We started to take my son Charles (Chucky) over so that he could learn to ride. It was the first time for me as well.

Once I was on the horse, Billy was behind me laughing so hard he almost fell off the horse he was on. I asked him what was so funny, and he said, "I don't know whose ass is bigger, yours or the horse's." And to that I say, both the horse and I looked quite good.

Billy was full of ideas. One day while riding along some train tracks, it started to rain. We found refuge in an abandoned boxcar, and while we were waiting for the rain to pass, we made love. When the rain was over, my cute but cheap outfit shrunk and was skintight. We cracked up because I thought I was cute in the outfit. We went straight home. I threw that pantsuit away, even though, obviously, that outfit clearly had some charm to it.

It was then that I found out Billy hadn't seen his boys for a while. I then took the initiative to ask his sons' mother, Sandra, about seeing his boys. I knew her in elementary school. She and I always liked each other as friends. It was tense, but we found common ground. She agreed as long as I was present. He got behind in child-support payments.

The boys were so happy. Chuck wanted brothers, and Sterling and Joe wanted the same. It was as if they were brothers from the start. People asked us if were we sure the boys weren't ours; they favored us so in appearance.

Everything seemed to be working out just fine when I found out that Billy still had baggage. He was trying to juggle relationships between Linda and I.

While this was happening, a friend of my mother's named Mary, who was more like an aunt or another mother, was going on a trip to the Bahamas with a group. My mother and I decided to go. I mentioned to Billy that I wanted to go, so he said he would pay for the trip for me. I knew this would give him a little more time to take care of his business and tie up loose ends with Linda. I accepted the offer to go since I had never been there.

We went to Nassau, Bahamas, for one glorious week. I was having fun, but most of the people were my mother's age. My mom and I were roommates. This was the best of arrangements. I became a little bored because of the age difference. We were invited to a soiree one night at the Nassau Beach hotel where we were staying. So Mama and I went. I love to dance, and I wiggled in my seat, waiting to be asked to dance by someone. A handsome, young man named

Vincent saw me and asked me if I knew how to do the reggae, a native dance done to the rhythm of steel-drum music. This was right up my alley. He started to teach me. I caught on quickly, and we wound up dancing exclusively all evening. At the end of the evening, he asked me to lunch the next day. I told him that I was there with my mother, and he said the invitation was for the two of us.

We not only had a wonderful lunch of native food, such as conch salad and conch fritters to name some; he took us on a tour of the island. It turned out he was born and raised right there on Nassau. We went to places that took my breath away with its beauty. We also went where tourists never went. It was like seeing a picture postcard come alive with us right in the midst. The weather was perfect, with hibiscus flowers in full bloom. The ocean was unbelievably blue, a light-azure with a sprinkle of turquoise. I never saw sand so clean before. Nassau was a far cry from Detroit, that was for sure.

The rest of the week, Vince would act as a tour guide and take me to different spots. Mama soon joined her friends away from us, and that was fine with us.

The time came for the trip to come to an end. Vincent and I developed a nice friendship, so we exchanged personal information and vowed to stay in touch with each other. He said that he came to the States a lot. That was when I found out that he was five years younger than I. He knew that there was someone in my life.

I returned to Detroit, and nothing changed with Billy. He still tried to get his business straight, so he said.

Vince started calling me and inviting me to come back to the island for the weekend. After about a month of conversation back and forth, there still was no change in Billy's situation. A year passed. I was tired of putting my life on hold for him.

I agreed to fly to Miami and meet Vince. He sent the ticket and some traveling money. He met me at the airport and had separate rooms for us at the Ambassador Suites Hotel in Miami. Each room was actually a suite with all the amenities: wine, cheese, flowers, and candy on my pillow. We spent most of the weekend talking and getting reacquainted. He wasn't seeing anyone at the time and expressed a very deep interest in me. He told me he was head accountant in charge of alcohol and beverages for the Nassau Beach Hotel, as well as other hotels. I liked him a lot. Waiting for Billy to make up his mind seemed useless at the time.

Vince started calling on a regular basis, asking me to be with him for the weekend. After a while, I gave in. He would have a ticket for me for a private plane to meet me in either Miami or Ft. Lauderdale. He was such a charismatic, warm gentleman he began to sweep me off my feet. I had the most romantic time of my life. All the things I read about and saw in the movies were now a part of my life. I was living a dream, flying away to the islands for the weekend on a regular basis. We danced, then strolled on the beach, met people, and just had lots of fun.

Vince, being a native Bahamian, had a few special places. One night he took me to a deserted spot on the beach, scooped out a large portion of the sand, and made love to me right there as the ocean rushed into the shore in the warm night breeze. This made me feel magical and timeless. So now I juggled two men in my life. It soon became more complicated than I could imagine. I now knew what Billy dealt with, for lack of a better term, and it wasn't easy. We both had investments of a sort. Well, the situation continued for approximately another year, with neither one of us pressing the other for a decision. We both knew in our hearts that the juggling and lying to each other was coming to an end. We still cared a lot about each other.

Vince and I became somewhat of an item. We talked about becoming engaged. Before I knew it, the time came to introduce him to Chucky and break all ties with Billy. Before this could happen, I had to break the news to Billy. I didn't look forward to the task.

Billy and I went to Sinbad's Seafood Restaurant down on the Detroit River one evening. He said that he had something to tell me, and I said the same to him. He asked for more time to take care of his business. That was when I broke my news to him. We had the longest, most painfully silent ride home afterward.

Billy and I again went our separate ways. Chucky, not knowing what was happening, swore that "It's a Shame" was written for me.

He came to really like Billy. He didn't accept my decision not to see Billy any more very well.

Vince and I continued to see each other. We became engaged and decided to set a wedding date. I was to formally meet his family, so I took Chucky with me. I had the time because I worked only ten months a year, so I could be off when Chucky was out of school for the summer. I was still working primarily for the Board of Education.

When we arrived in Nassau. Some friends met us and remarked how happy they were to meet my brother. They gave us an engagement party. After more comments of a similar nature, I stopped the music and announced to everyone that Chucky was my son and not my brother. I later found out that Vince told them that I was bringing my little brother. It was clear that my having a child embarrassed him.

This was the beginning of the end to that relationship. I also found out that after we were to be married, Vince made arrangements (without my knowledge) for Chucky to attend school in Germany, away from us. This led to a huge argument, the end result being a broken engagement. We returned to the States, and Chucky and I went on with our lives. Vince tried to patch things up, but I realized that I never really loved him. I got caught up in the glamour and the excitement of the moment.

Billy and I kept in touch. We started to date again. He was a little angry and heartbroken because of the moves I made. I suspected his ego was bruised because he helped to pay for the initial trip. He told me I broke his heart, not realizing that if he took care of business at the very start, things might have happened entirely differently. What about my heart and my ego? He never faced the fact that he was keeping me hanging on. It was all about him and how he felt. He never considered his participation in this little fiasco. From that moment on, Billy couldn't stand the record "Nassau's Gone Funky Now," or reggae music. Anything to do with any tropical island was highly disturbing to him. We resolved our issues, I thought. We let bygones be bygones.

We went back to the same seafood restaurant in downtown Detroit to make sure everything was resolved. Billy poured his heart out and let me know he wanted a relationship with me and that everything was straight with him. He lied. Oh boy, was I the queen of being naive! I went back to work, and things were great! I didn't know that his situation with the girl had not changed. I mean, they weren't still living together, but they were still involved. He was still trying to get her with The Supremes, he later said.

One day after work, I happened to be driving past the apartment building in which he supposedly helped get her an apartment, and I spotted his car. I always had a photographic memory; I remembered his license plate number. Later when I told him I saw his car there. He denied it until I told him the license plate number. His response was, "How the hell did you remember that?" This would be the first of many such incidents. Little did I know what was in store for me.

Billy was a master at game playing. He had to acquire those skills in order to survive the music industry. He could manipulate people very well. I went from a leisurely, somewhat middle-class way of life to a life with a man with one pair of summer shoes on in the winter, one suit that was too small, and a gift of gab. Time and the road did a job on Billy. I still saw him as my roller-skating partner of years ago. Like I said, I was so naive. Can I say right here, though, so was he! We met our proverbial Waterloo!

I made moves in other areas in the meantime. While Billy and I dated, I bought a home that just happened to be down the street from Marvin Gaye. The house was an HUD (Housing and Urban Development) house, and I had to offer a bid to the government in order to purchase it.

I made a bid, and it was refused. I was told that my credit was such that I would qualify for a house in the ghetto. At the time, I had a girlfriend who worked in real estate. She quietly informed me of an experiment that was currently taking place in Detroit and a few other cities. The housing authority bought homes in upper-middle-class neighborhoods for welfare families, subsidizing the rent and keeping up the properties.

When I found this out, I wrote a letter to the Head of the Housing Administration (George Romney, ex-governor of Michigan), letting them know that I knew about the trial experiment that was being conducted in Detroit. I wrote that I did not think that as a working mother, I should have to be forced to buy and live in such an undesirable area of the city, while my taxes were paying for welfare families that were being placed in better housing than I.

I received a nasty answer. They wrote:

> The Welfare Housing was an experiment that did *not* work. You currently have a bid in for a house on Greenlawn. Just wait and see what happens!

Of course, the bid went through, and my credit was fine.

Billy and I now dated on a steady basis. He was going to New York one weekend for a gig at the Apollo Theatre. He invited me to meet him there because he would be driving The Temptation's limousine to make extra money and thought I would enjoy the ride back, plus be company for him. The Spinners were performing on the same bill with The Temptations and the O'Jays, among other acts.

When I arrived in New York, there was no Billy to meet me at the airport, so I took a taxicab to the Apollo because he said he would be there if he wasn't at the airport. Upon my arrival at the theatre, I met a huge crowd that was in a near riot state. I thought the crowd was anxious to get in. I didn't know they stormed the box office. I told the driver to take me to the backstage entrance. He was so scared he collected his fare and left me standing there. I couldn't get close to the door, and there was no Billy in sight. So I proceeded to go through the crowd, down the street to the nearest hotel, with my luggage in one hand and mink stole over the other. I wondered why the people sort of parted and let me through with no problem.

When I finally got Billy on the telephone, he asked where I was. He told me to hurry up and return to the backstage door, and he would meet me there. When I got there, everybody laughed, and I didn't know why. I was mad because I went through so much to get there. Billy finally stopped laughing and told me the people must have taken me for an undercover person, in other words, a "police plant," because I survived the stroll through the mob unscathed. Well, after everybody had their fun, I met the O'Jays, The Temptations, and a man they called Shaky Jimmy (Billy's buddy). When the show was over, the rest of The Spinners flew back to Detroit, with the exception of Pervis, who rode in the backseat of the limo.

My next trip with Billy was to the Regal Theatre in Chicago. The Spinners had a band by the name The Nite Liters. Billy hired the group, and they were supposed to get paid right after the show. Billy was so busy paying everybody after the show the theatre was closing, and I was still in the audience waiting. When it finally dawned on him where I was, he came back for me. He apologized profusely and said that he got so busy it totally slipped his mind that I was waiting for him. Needless to say, I was shook by being in a town all alone, depending on someone who would forget my presence. This showed me that he wasn't used to taking anyone out on the road with him. I started taking control of my own needs when I was out with him. After a while, I sensed deep down Billy was somehow trying to show me that he was not going to be outdone by Vince.

I must say that going with Billy was exciting and interesting, watching him wheel and deal for the group in order to get things done and to get paid on top of it. It was different from being pampered by Vince. I wanted to give Billy a chance because I believed and loved him and the rest of the guys from childhood. Billy was a real hustler, as far as the group was concerned. I admired that in him.

My very first trip to Washington, DC, was when The Spinners and The Four Tops appeared at the Howard Theatre. It was a great show, but I wanted to see the White House—where the president of the United States of America lived of course. I am sort of a historian in that I try to take in historical sites wherever I go. Well, would you believe, after the show, there was a crap game between some of the Tops, some of The Spinners, and Billy's buddy from New York, Shaky Jimmy. Yes, a crap game! Aretha called the group her crap-shooting Spinners. Billy was right in the center of it all. I sat and waited patiently for him to finish. He was losing at first and asked me for my return airline ticket. I looked at him like he just lost his mind. Reluctantly, I gave it to him and walked away. He assured me that he knew what he was doing. A little later, he called me over and gave me at least $5,000 (five thousand) dollars. I don't remember exactly how much there was because he said to put it away where no one else knew where it was. I stuffed the money in my bra.

We left later that night to see the White House. It was around three thirty in the morning. The White-House guard questioned us as to why we were there so late. Billy told him he didn't have time to bring me before the show, and he couldn't take me back to Detroit in peace until I had been there. I found out much later that Shaky Jimmy gave him some loaded dice and taught Billy how to switch them. This was when I learned the strange fondness to which they gave out nicknames. I asked him how they could call that man Shaky—because he was suffering with cerebral palsy, an illness that caused him to shake. Billy said nobody paid that any attention; they were too busy watching for his slick, crafty moves. There was also a lame fellow that they all called Cripple George, who also was a gambling friend of Billy's. I never had the nerve to call those fellows by those titles.

When we got back to Detroit, Billy put most of the money down on a car. He always said, "The Four Tops paid the down payment for his car." I got my share for my participation.

It was not all fun and games, this life with an entertainer. Billy still had child-support problems. When I got my income tax refund, I paid the arrears so that he could continue to pursue his career. It kept him out of jail and free to maneuver. Even though they had a hit record out, there was still no real money because Motown said The Spinners owed them. That was what Billy told me.

Among all the problems, the guys in the group needed transportation. Billy, being their ambassador, knew that I had good credit. He asked me to cosign for a station wagon.

He asked me, "How much do you love me?"

My answer was, "Why?"

He answered with, "The group needs a way to get to and from gigs," and I would use my credit to help them.

As I stated before, they were all like my brothers, and I knew them almost all of my life. Most of all, I believed in them, so fool that

I was, I signed. This was the beginning of my credit being ruined. They never worked steady enough to make the payments on time.

Back in those days, they paid how they could at the time, I suppose. Not long after the loan, Paul Williams of The Temptations died, and The Spinners asked their mates to prepare some food to help the family out after the funeral. We responded and helped out. We were more than happy to do so.

Life was good, and I still worked the three jobs and made ends meet, including paying some of the notes on the station wagon. Then one day, I went with Yvonne, Bobby's girlfriend and my close friend, to her furrier, and I fell in love with fur (this was before animal rights). I made a deal with Art Bricker, the furrier, to get a sable-trimmed mink coat. It was the most beautiful coat I had ever seen. It was a blonde mink with brown sable trim and lined with eighteen-karat gold threaded lining. The bottom of the coat zipped off and became a stole, while the top was a three-quarter-length jacket. I had a dress made of the lining material to match the coat.

My father went with me at a later date to see it and signed for me to get it. That was when I learned in such elegant, grand fashion that The Spinners ruined my credit.

Before I go much further, let me tell you how The Spinners came to be with Motown. When I saw Billy again after the long span between childhood and adulthood, The Spinners had a few hit records, namely "Truly Yours," "For All We Know," and "That's What Girls Are Made For," on the Tri-Phi label before they signed with Motown. Harvey Fuqua of the group, The Moonglows, was the owner of that label and also their manager. At a later time, he married Gwen Gordy (Berry's sister) and merged with Motown. After a while, Harvey and Gwen were divorced. This was how, according to Billy, The Spinners came to be with Motown.

They were with Motown a number of years before their biggest hit record, "It's a Shame." Motown never acknowledged how really big the record hit. Shortly after the record hit, the lead singer, G. C. Cameron, left to pursue a solo career.

In addition to losing a lead singer and holding auditions, it soon became time for The Spinners to re-sign with Motown. They decided against it for various reasons, one being they always felt they were treated as second class there. It was a frustrating decade for them. Motown wanted to let them go without their professional name.

Billy was very angry and complained about it. I suggested that he see an attorney. I introduced him to my attorney. He read their contract and decided to help them. He knew someone at Motown. He negotiated for The Spinners, and Billy left with their professional name. I suggested to him that he register the assumed name. I then went with him to register the assumed name (I still have the original documentation where he alone owned the name). Sometime later, Billy decided to put everybody's name on the assumed name because in his mind, it would help to keep the group unified. He wanted to be fair with the group, plus give them additional incentive to stay together. Because he started the group, he felt responsible for them. Without their professional name, their career would be disastrous.

Now that they were available, it was time for a new recording contract and new management. Times were tough for the group because of the transitions. Somehow these problems drew Billy and me closer.

After Motown, Philippe Wynn was selected as the replacement singer. Rehearsals were often at my house. By this time, Billy moved in, and we paid the deposit for my mother to have her own apartment away from the chaos; she still worked. Everybody rehearsed there: the band and whoever Billy had to rehearse. Sometimes rehearsals would end the dawn of the following day. In fact, I remember the neighbors wanting to come over while they were rehearsing. I told them, "Only if I can go over to your house for some peace and quiet."

Work got so scarce the group threatened to break up. One day Billy called Aretha Franklin and told her that he was losing his guys. They needed work. He asked her if she could help him out. Within a few days, Ruth Bowen, Aretha's manager, called Billy and soon made arrangements for The Spinners to work with Aretha. She suggested that they go with Atlantic Records, where she was at the time. The Spinners worked steady with Aretha for approximately a year. She was and still is a true, dear friend, truly The Queen.

At Atlantic Records, a producer by the name of Thom Bell was given a list of artists to produce, and his choice was The Spinners. He had quite a few hits on such artists as The Delfonics (La La), just to name one group and many more, with his smooth "Sound of Philadelphia." Thom came to my house and sat down at my piano and recorded each of The Spinner's voices. He returned to Philadelphia and began to come up with tunes that were tailor-made for The Spinners' sound.

Thom introduced Billy to Buddy Allen, who also came to my house to meet with Billy and the group about becoming their manager. This was in 1971. Buddy's wife, Connee, and their son, Steve, were very involved with Buddy Allen Management. I liked the idea of it being a family affair.

Thom Bell said to the group, "Next year, you'll be number one."

In 1972 The Spinners' song "I'll Be Around" began a string of top 20 and no. 1 R and B hits and gold records that included "Could It Be I'm Falling in Love," "Mighty Love, Then Came You," and "The Rubberband Man." After hearing what Thom did, I had to agree that the man knew his stuff. The Spinners didn't believe that "Rubberband Man" was going to be a hit record. Thom and The Spinners were a winning combination, leading to five gold albums and several gold singles.

Billy and I had dated for four years now. One day Chucky asked him when he was going to marry his mother. Billy's remark was, "Sure, man, I'm going to make her an honest woman." Then he laughed. After that, we began to talk seriously about marriage. I asked Billy if The Spinners always came first in his book. His answer was yes because this was his livelihood. In fact, he said the fellows had an unwritten agreement between them that no woman, be it wife or otherwise, would come between them and their career. The Spinners singing group always came first.

I respected his answer, although I might not have agreed with it. With both of us having been married before, I understood where he came from. I did appreciate his honesty.

Well, we decided it was finally time to get married, so we decided to go and apply for the license. He asked me to quit work.

The timing was right! I quit! Another problem rose. Billy had a phobia about being at city hall. He said that each time that he was there before concerning child-support payments, he was sent to jail. We argued about it and eventually worked it out and got the license. We went out to dinner from there. I was so confused about the whole thing I placed my order, and when the food came, I couldn't eat. I suddenly lost my appetite. That was when I began to realize that hardly anything bothered Billy. He ate his and my dinner. Nothing could spoil his dinner or life itself. Ever.

We kept the license until it was due to expire. Then on November 26, 1972, we went to a cabaret dance. I wore a gown that was low-cut with thigh high splits on either side, not exactly wedding attire.

Billy said, "Let's go over to Cecil and Earline's and ask Cecil to marry us."

It was about one o'clock in the morning. It just so happened that they were home. When we called them about marrying us, they thought we were kidding. They then told us to come on over. When we got there, Cecil said we needed witnesses. Billy said to call Phil and Beverly Wooldridge. (Phil Wooldridge was The Spinners' business manager.) When the Wooldridges arrived, Cecil went and got his Bible and started the "traditional" ceremony.

When he came to the part that said, "Love, honor, and obey," Billy said, "Hold it! Would you repeat that please?"

When Cecil came to the section of the marital vows that said, "Giving all your worldly endowments," I said, "Hold it! Would you repeat that please?"

Beverly started to cry, and I wanted to know what she was crying about. She said she had never been to a wedding before. I told her she still hadn't. We went on with it, giving her a front-row seat to what would be a fiasco. One sign came when we went home. I expected a romantic wedding night and put on a sexy gown.

Billy looked at me and said, "Let's wait until this Audie Murphy movie is over."

We had been living together for three months, so I guess I had already had my honeymoon. There was nothing traditional about my marriage right from the start. He didn't tell me Audie Murphy came after The Spinners being first. This would be the first of many surprises. One surprise I appreciated was that before we got married, Billy did tell me that he would be my last husband, I would never be bored, and I had to quit my jobs. I was more than happy to quit working. I was thirty-four, and Billy was nine months younger, thirty-three. He used to tease me and say I was robbing the cradle. I told him the cradle was the oldest cradle I ever knew of. I wasn't as naive as before either. Knowing that I was marrying an entertainer, I asked him to not bring anything home except him and his money, and the state of Michigan would be mine. He had the whole world to deal with as far as women. I didn't have to know about it.

The next evening, he did take me to see Lena Horne. She was performing across the Detroit River in Windsor, Canada, at the Elmwood Casino. We went backstage and met her. I just finished reading her book; she signed her copy of her autobiography for me and said that she was happy for us and a little jealous. She just recently lost her husband. She looked at me and told me to be as happy as she had been in her marriage. Lena Horne was the kindest, most gracious person, as well as a very classy entertainer, whom I enjoyed tremendously.

Some of the trappings of success started showing up here and there. We began to fix up the HUD home. Billy and I were out one evening and passed a furniture store named Art Van. We saw the perfect set of furniture for the house. Billy promised to buy it when he became famous and was making money enough to pay cash for the whole set as we saw it. Somehow I believed him.

Did he keep his word? Yes! Yes! Yes! Let me explain. First, by the time we bought the furniture, we had to wait until it came from Canada on special order. There was a couch with the end tables attached. The color was magenta with silver end tables, a round comfort chair with a silver base; silver lamps on the end tables, and finally, in the dining room a huge glass top table standing on a huge silver base with a matching silver china cabinet. (It took at least four men to lift the glass top alone.) I went out and found a bar-shaped-like fireplace; it was built with silver-and-gold panels and opened to expose the bar. It hung on the wall in the living room. The record player was a large cabinet that was a fake fireplace that lit up with fake logs, and if you lifted the top, there was the record player.

The floor was covered with pink shag carpet, which was all the rage in the seventies. A mirrored glass wall in the dining room highlighted, where all of his gold records and the star from the Hollywood Walk of Fame were hung.

Now let me describe our bedroom! It started out as an attic! We decided we needed a larger room, and we both had some ideas about what we wanted. We met a guy named Dickey, who did some work for a friend. I called him. Billy had to leave town, so it was left up to me to get the room done. Dickey and his crew started immediately! One night I was looking at the stars, and the next night, the frame for the room was complete.

There was a closet that went the entire width of the house. I remember when Billy came home, he told Dickey to put some shelves in the middle, or else all the closet would wind up being mine. That was a smart move. Next came the bathroom with a black sink, bathtub, shower. and toilet, with gold-colored faucet and fixtures.

Finally, a king-size bed was placed on a platform that Dickey made. On each side of the bed was a panel that lit up with various buttons. With the buttons, you could see who was at the front door (on a television that hung from the ceiling) and buzz whoever was there into the house. Then you could buzz the door to the bedroom. In the panels were drawers. We kept our marijuana there. You could turn on the mirrored ball that hung over our bed next to the plastic-mirrored, ceiling-large panel.

Over in the corner was a fountain with colored lights when it was turned on. Billy loved the rain-like sound of water. The room was soundproof!

Next to the bed was a mini refrigerator. When you ascended the stairs leading to the bedroom, there was a painted mural of a woman with a goat's head trying to hold on with a long leash to a large lion. Lightning flashed all around in the painting.

Astrology was a big thing in the seventies. I was supposed to be a Capricorn (the goat), and Billy was a Leo (the lion). I found out later that the mural was an exact image of my life. This was something else I knew nothing about. He studied astrology! Billy always told me that you could be an expert in a subject of which the other person had no knowledge.

One day I had the laugh of my life! Billy and I argued about something. I don't know what the argument was about. Billy decided to tip the fountain over because I bought it.

I sat in the middle of the bed and started to laugh. He looked at me quizzically. One part of the fountain weighed two hundred pounds without the water in it. He struggled, huffing and puffing! Then when it wouldn't move, he started to laugh too!

We had fun with the fountain. One time we filled it with champagne and drank from it.

Billy had a singing group of men called Powerful Source (Harold, Linwood, Nate, and Jack), and they could really sing. Billy tried to help them, but his career took all his time. Well, one of the fellows had a brother in art school. Our favorite song was Donna Summer's "MacArthur Park" at that time. We decided to have the part of the song that said, "And my passion flows like rivers through the sky," painted on the door of the bathroom because it faced the bed. Keith, an artist and brother of Harold of Powerful Source, took a picture of me and a picture of Billy and created the illusion of us standing nude from the waist up hugging each other while standing water. Keith was quite good and later became a wonderful graphic artist, if I remember correctly.

One of The Spinners had a girlfriend who worked for Pan American Airlines. She had a pair of gorgeous Lhasa Apso dogs. The female had puppies. Delores, the owner, gave Bobby one, and Billy and me one. We named our dog Brightie because we saw Delores in Brighton, England, although she lived in the states. Bobby's dog was named Sadie, after The Spinners' record.

The Lhasa Apso was a special breed of dog that was traditionally given away in pairs.

Small dogs with long hair, they were bred to guard the temples in parts of Tibet. What I found especially interesting was that they don't shed and have the bark of a large dog. They are very smart, but also quite stubborn. To top it off, they also tend to take on their owner's personality! Billy said the dog spent most of her time with me, so she was mostly like me (she might have been somewhat confused).

We got her when she was six weeks old. She was the cutest fur ball. Later, on the days that she was groomed and her rhinestone collar was placed on her, she acted as if she was being shown in a dog show.

I took her to buy a bed, and she went to the most expensive one in the store, which was made of oak. I bought a fake fur coat to match one of mine. She even flew first class with us (well, perhaps she was like me to an extent). If anyone walked near our house, she barked.

One day I let her out in the backyard to use the bathroom (the one day I didn't walk her). Just like the Disney movie *Lady and the Tramp*, she got pregnant by the neighborhood's scruffiest, unclean, no-shots dog, a tramp named Chief. We never thought about having her spayed.

I was so angry I wanted to shoot that dog! Then I realized it was my fault. If I had not broken my routine, perhaps this wouldn't have happened, but I also believed that whatever was supposed to be would be!

We had such fun during the first few years of marriage. Marvin Gaye and his wife at the time lived down the street. Edward of Gladys Knight's Pips lived a few blocks away. One the Four Tops lived in Palmer Woods not far away, and his daughter was a friend of one our sons. This was Detroit! Anyone famous could be your neighbor.

I traveled with Billy quite frequently. My first trip to Los Angeles, California, was so exciting. The second trip, it was, shall we say, pleasurable business. Billy and I met with a fabulous clothing designer by the name of Harvey Krantz and his wife, Yeta (we are still dear friends to this day). Harvey designed uniforms for almost anybody who was somebody famous. He dressed The Oak Ridge Boys, Glenn Campbell, The Temptations, KC and the Sunshine Band, Hank Snow, Sergio Mendez & Brazil '66, George Foreman, Johnny Mathis, Little Anthony and the Imperials, Roy Clark, and James Brown, just to name a few. The Spinners started wearing Harvey's clothing and still donned his designs. His designs have spanned the years and in step with the fashion transformations of the times. You could say his clothing line was timeless. Harvey's look completed The Spinners' success.

On that trip, we stayed at the Holiday Inn on Highland Avenue. This was where Bob Hope usually was in the evenings. We met him at the revolving restaurant at the top of the hotel. He was a very wonderful, gracious man. I also met one of the Harlem Globetrotters by the name of Goose Tatum. He truly was a delight to meet.

It was a strange sensation, to just encounter famous personalities almost everywhere you looked. We saw Glenn Ford, a world-renowned movie star, at The Farmers Market (a famous, awe-inspiring place).

One of the most interesting people was Adele Astaire, the sister of Fred Astaire. She told me over lunch that she and Fred danced together as children on shows until the motion picture industry signed Fred and not her.

This exposure allowed me to branch out into other interests as well. While I was staying at the Holiday Inn, I just happened to visit the hotel gift shop. While there, I saw a tester and bought a fruit-flavored deodorant body spray named Macho. There was a complete line of this Macho, including strawberry soap on a rope, three different fragrances of cologne. Also, there was strawberry shampoo and conditioner. The line of products was made with all-natural ingredients. It was the most fascinating men's line I ever saw. My mind started turning! I got in touch with the Jordan K. Rand Company, the owners of the product. I found out there was no Jordan K. Rand. This was an assumed name for the product. There actually were two brothers who had come up with the idea and had it on trial in the gift shop.

I talked it over with Billy and thought because it was so new I could try to get in on the ground floor with the brothers. I did what research I could, and I finally made contact and set up a meeting with them. They just won an award for their packaging. One of them was a terrific artist, and the other was very knowledgeable in marketing. Billy and I went to see their laboratory and offices.

After getting acquainted and discussing our ideas, they agreed to send me a shipment of everything they had in stock on consignment.

I needed something to do after working three jobs. Billy didn't see my getting involved with selling Macho as a job. He figured it would keep me busy and allow me to be available when he needed me. I had so much fun promoting this product! The flavored body deodorant sprays were the most fun. I had booths at trade shows, state fairs, department stores, and wherever I could. The women tasted it after I sprayed it on their hands, then they called their husbands over. The marketing techniques, including the displays, were so sophisticated and classy the people who stopped and were interested whispered, snickered, blushed, and bought.

It was a very hot item with the entertainers. Billy was my top salesperson. The company had six flavors when I started: strawberry, lemon, fruit ambrosia, chocolate, lime, and licorice. I suggested and got three more: pineapple, tropical, and coconut.

I remember Billy said that Johnny of The Dells said to him, "Just call me the Lemonade Man."

It wasn't long before I became the top distributor, the only female, and the only Afro-American. My boys were young and out of high school now. They went to the trade shows and different places to help me. The Macho proved to be great for generating income, as well as a tax write-off, because I housed it in my basement and literally worked from home.

Having been a bookkeeper helped. I had a staff of salespersons spanning cities such as Detroit, Indianapolis, Ohio, Minneapolis, Kentucky, and Washington, DC.

That lasted for a few years. Then the brothers who owned Jordan K. Rand decided to split, and consequently, their business went under. I was able to continue with my sales for a few years more due to the inventory I had on hand.

During these times, I began smoking. Cigarettes were being glamorized. They were made thinner and in pretty colors with gold filter tips. Cigarette holders were long and chic. I was attracted to all the above. This was all part of the classy ultrafeminine look being shown in the movies. Going to the movies was an escape for a lot of people back then and still is. Billy was already smoking. It wasn't long before Billy and I were not only smoking cigarettes, but marijuana as well. He said it would help me to relax and not be so stressed. I never knew what he meant until much later in our marriage. Oh boy, did the stress come! Billy was a character!

Gold records started happening for the guys rather quickly. The first gold record, "I'll Be Around," was presented to them at the Twenty Grand Club in Detroit. I was glad Billy's mother, Nelly, lived to see his accomplishment. I can recall buying her a dress for the occasion. She was overjoyed. She remarked to me, "Honey, for what you paid for one dress, I would have bought three." I smiled because I had just spent one hundred dollars.

Nelly was so very proud of her firstborn. She suffered a debilitating form of rheumatoid arthritis. She was a brave, kind, loving, gentle soul. I loved her dearly. I could see her in the softer side of Billy. Unfortunately, she would never see any more of his achievements. We lost her not long after we were married. We buried her in the dress she became so fond of.

Things happened very fast. Atlantic Records had a press party for The Spinners and their wives in New York. We really received carte-blanche treatment. The champagne flowed. Everything was all so exciting and glamorous. That night, we met Ahmet Ertegun, the then president of the Atlantic Records.

One of the promoters responsible for the records hitting and becoming gold was and still is my cherished friend, Barbara Harris. She did a fantastic job and was at the top of her game in those days. Billy was a generous man, but very cunning. He showered me with expensive clothing and shoes. If he liked something, he bought it in every color, especially shoes. He knew the story about me as a child being the smallest and sometimes getting hand-me-downs from my sisters. I had a real weakness for new clothes.

I noticed that he studied a person's personality. Over a period of time, I learned that there was always a method to his madness. My real life lesson began, and I was quite unaware. Any weakness exposed was his playground, or you might say, his power over you. I never imagined this happening with my husband, or my concept of a husband. He was my other half, my protector, I thought.

The first major television show that I attended with The Spinners had its highs and lows. It was *The Merv Griffin Show* in Los Angeles, California. During the performance, for some reason, the audience was very unresponsive. I sat down front and noticed the deadpan expressions and watched gazing. Oh no, we could not have this going on. I began to rock my head to the beat and mouth the lyrics to "I'll Be Around" and "How Could I Let You Get Away" (their two-sided hit), as if to show the platinum-haired host's audience what they were missing. At the very least, I hoped to encourage the guys.

The resistance from the audience was easier to understand when later—while The Spinners were changing—I met Merv Griffin and Tony Randall, one half of the *Odd Couple* TV duo. Randall frowned and said to me, "I have never heard of The Spinners. I watched and listened because you were having such a great time."

It occurred to me that the audience were of a social set that may not be as hip and up-to-date as the people I was used to. Randall then introduced me to Jack Klugman, who was smoking a cigarette. Tony remarked that he was trying to get Jack to quit smoking. Jack said, "Fat chance." Meeting them in the green room was the highlight of the night.

When the money started coming in on a regular basis and increased, Billy gave me the option of traveling with him, or buying a bigger house. To me, the house wasn't as important as seeing new places with him. I opted traveling with him. Tickled with my response, he said to me, "I am going to be your last husband."

Billy didn't seem to get the message about my wanting to travel with them. The Spinners' first overseas trip was to London, England. I didn't go, and my telephone bill was around eight hundred dollars. I suppose I got my point across more convincingly because after that trip, I started going upon invitation from Billy. I made myself a promise that I would not call him or show up anywhere uninvited. If he wanted to talk to me, he would call. And the same went for me being with him on his gigs. He would have to send for me. After all, this was his job.

I was overjoyed that Billy now asked me to go with him to various places. He told me that every place was just a gig for him until I came into his life. It somehow reminded me of skating backward in his arms back at the Duke. As I said earlier, I am a historian of sorts. I enjoyed being in places I had read and studied about when I was younger. I got word that more international travel was coming, so I got a passport so I would be ready.

Wouldn't you know, another trip to London, England, was scheduled, and Billy invited me to go! I barely contained the excitement. Just the thought of the trip was overwhelming! It was then that I found out that I was the only wife going. This was even more exciting! I felt a sense of loss for the other wives because they would be missing such a great experience. I must admit that sad feeling didn't last long; I recovered rather quickly.

The flight over to England was the longest that I had ever been on. I was so thrilled; sleep was hard to come by. Upon arrival, we were met by representatives from the Atlantic Record Company of England. They put us in sleek, black limousines called Daimlers.

I asked, "What kind of car is a Daimler?"

I was told these were special cars, manufactured once a year for the queen of England. They were bulletproof and had two large gas tanks, with tinted windows. The interior was fabulous and very roomy with wooden trim. Of course, this was another first for me. The chauffeur had only driven royalty and certain dignitaries. I didn't know how The Spinners felt, but I felt majestic and light-headed with privilege.

We kept quarters at one of the best hotels in London. In the afternoon, it is customary for everything to be placed on hold for tea time. I finally was able to enjoy the celebrated tea and crumpets (lightly toasted griddle cakes) I heard about as a child. History came alive with me being an active, willing participant. Life became a wonderful dream come true!

The Spinners had a lot to do: press conferences, meet and greets, etc. We had an assigned chauffeur, Fred, during our stay. The

Spinners let Billy and I have our own driver since I was with him. So on that first day, which was a free day for the guys, Billy hired him to take us on a tour of sorts.

The driver took us to see Buckingham Palace. What a sight! The queen's personal guard went through their paces on the grounds, so the driver told the head guard who we were and asked if I could film them. I was glad I brought a movie camera along. The next stop was Number 10 Downing Street, where Winston Churchill had lived. Our final stop before downtown London was Wellington Park, which wasn't far from Buckingham Palace. The tour was a living piece of history for me. There were parts of building that were still standing, being remnants of World-War-II bombings, so the driver said. Billy was interested because it was a different country, and I was thrilled just to be there. He soon became bored with the sightseeing and was ready to return to the hotel. This was when the tour ended for the day. Both Billy and I were anxious to try fish and chips. That was our dinner for the evening.

Atlantic Records had a most pleasant surprise for us the following evening. We were invited to Chelsea, England, to a delightful place named Chelsea's Rendezvous. This was our first experience tasting the most exquisite, exotic dishes including Peking duck, sesame prawns, and fried seaweed, just for starters. The service was fit for royalty. While we ate, the waiters changed the linen, as it was becoming soiled. We never missed a stroke eating our meal. The table cloth was being rolled up and replaced with a fresh table cloth and fresh napkins. It was the most amazing feat I have witnessed to this day. While we enjoyed ourselves, we soon realized that the drivers who drove us there stood outside of their cars, waiting for us. Some of The Spinners asked that they be invited inside. We were told that they could wait in the kitchen with the help.

I would have the same type fare with Billy both in Los Angeles, California, and Manhattan, New York, at a place called Mr. Chows. As Billy said, "You could throw a dart at the menu with your eyes closed and never pick a loser." While we had this splendid evening, the head waiter or owner decided that I would be his fare. I thought he was interesting, but he was not concerned with the fact that I was there with my husband.

On the next trip to London, we went to Chelsea's Rendezvous and dined as before. Santro, the head waiter or owner invited Billy and me to his flat after dinner. We accepted the invitation for after-dinner drinks. I told Billy about his previous flirting. A woman was there. Upon inquiry, we found out that she was his mistress. She began to play folk music on her guitar, while Santro knelt in front of me and proceeded to take my shoes off. Billy just watched and didn't say a word to Santro. I spoke up and told him that I would kick his teeth out if he continued. Needless to say, he got the message. When we left, I asked Billy why he didn't stop the man. Billy said he didn't know what the man was doing, and he was just waiting to see what was going to happen next. This incident, fortunately, was controllable.

By the time the next trip to London came around, I was still the only wife going. He kept his promise to take me along. I had my own chauffeur, so I shopped at Harrods, which was world famous. It was the most magnificent place that had the largest variety of eclectic shops. I saw a white gabardine raincoat in a Vogue magazine while there. You better believe I purchased it. Then I saw some baggy boots in several colors of leather. Of course I bought every color. I remember it began to rain that day. The chauffeur was there with an umbrella to protect me and my packages. I never felt a drop of rain. It was simply wonderful! Now I experienced some of how the wealthy were treated.

A reporter named Denise Hall, who worked for an R and B magazine there, met with me that day. She and I became quick friends. After her interview with The Spinners, she invited me to her home for a visit. The Spinners would be going to Liverpool to perform and on to Scotland. Denise was from Colchester (the oldest recorded city in the United Kingdom), which wasn't far from either place. Colchester was where the Colchester siege took place in the year 1648. According to historians, people starved and resorted to eating cats and dogs in order to survive after a civil war.

I accepted her invitation. Later we took the train from London to Colchester. I don't remember how long the trip was because Denise and I talked all the way. When we arrived in Colchester, Denise's sister was waiting for us with a taxicab.

Well, she thought she spotted her boyfriend with another girl in a taxi and suddenly yelled to the cab driver, "Follow that cab!"

After finding that it was not her boyfriend, Denise and I looked at each other, laughed, and we both said, "I have always wanted to say, 'Follow that cab!'"

This day was when the real England adventure began. The next stop was at Denise's home. I was very impressed. Their home was filled with nostalgia and antiques. It was very British, which I had never seen before. It was furnished with things left to them by their deceased parents.

Denise's daughter was waiting for us. Her name was Amber, a fetching little girl between nine or ten years of age and very beautiful. I suggested that we do some grocery shopping. This was to be quite a different venture.

We went to a grocery store and took Amber with us. I never knew that the so-called common folk only had so little to spend. I proceeded to pick out what I thought was needed for an American meal, which I expected to prepare. As I shopped, Denise was afraid that she would not have enough money for what I selected. I noticed her fretting, so I let her know that not only was I preparing dinner, I would also be buying whatever they desired. Amber coyly asked her mother for some biscuits. I told Denise, by all means, to let her have what she wanted. That was when I found out biscuits meant cookies. Being with them was such an education.

Dinner went well! I prepared fried chicken, salad, and pan-fried potatoes with onions. Detroit had come to England! Afterward we got better acquainted and discussed plans for the rest of my visit with them. Amber suggested that I sleep in her bed during my stay. I felt honored. Amber's bed was so soft and cozy. She had a goose down comforter. Once you snuggled in for the night, you immediately fell asleep. I felt like Goldilocks of *The Three Bears*—I had the best bed of all.

The next day was to be filled with a tour of the town and some shopping. The weather was perfect. Rain had been in the forecast for the day, but we were greeted with the sun. After we had breakfast, I donned my walking shoes, took my movie camera, and anxiously awaited the day's events. It was impossible to capture it all on film! I barely contained myself.

We started with the Colchester Castle. It was an original site—a remainder of the Roman days built by the Romans. It even had a moat. I had never seen a real castle, much less entered one. The first thing I noticed was it was cold and somewhat damp inside because it was almost all made of stone so that even though it was a warm spring day, the warmth couldn't penetrate the walls. There was also a dungeon. We couldn't see it because it was being repaired. Being there in the castle made the historical event of the Colchester siege more real with me. When we left the castle, we noticed that there was some excavation going on. We went to investigate and noticed a large section of tiled pavement setting to one side. I took movies of it and recognized the date, 110 AD, carved into it. Upon inquiry, we were told it was part of a Roman street. 110 AD, can you imagine that? In England, nothing can be destroyed or built without the permission of the queen. Almost anything that is discovered could be of some historical significance.

Denise decided that we should continue on our venture. I was in seventh heaven! We visited a few small boutiques. There was this adorable, quaint, little hat shop. Being the hat and gloves collector that I was, I practically bought every hat in the store. I still have a couple. After my purchases, the shop closed for the day. Apparently, I bought her out.

A bobby (British for policeman) passed by as we left the shop. I asked if I could take a movie of him. He smiled and said with a heavy British intonation, "Yes, I would be happy to be in your film." His accent was so crisp and proper.

Our day of adventure was coming to a close. I suddenly realized that the next day I would be leaving for Liverpool, England. I wanted to purchase some chicken and fish to cook for members of the upcoming show. The fish market was not far from where we were. Every place was inside easy proximity of each other. To go from one place to the other was within strolling distance.

In the fish market, I purchased so much fish the owners had to close. They had never done so much business in one day before. Boy, were they happy! It was the same scenario when we bought chicken at the grocery store. The amusing part about the whole day was nobody had any bags. I noticed people putting things in their pockets and began to wonder. Nobody ever bought in such quantities. There were no grocery-store baggers.

Saddened by the thought of leaving Colchester; I prepared myself mentally and physically for the next stage of my exciting adventure. Denise and I froze the chicken and fish. I was so happy she and I would be traveling together. She had a column to write, and I was anxious to see Billy again. We spent quite a bit of time on the telephone.

We took another train ride to Liverpool the following day. We arrived in the late afternoon. I didn't know what to expect in Liverpool. Liverpool produced such timeless talent as The Beatles. It was a dreary little town. I don't remember where the performance took place. The audience seemed to be more than the town's capacity. There was a sort of high-pitch electricity in the air, almost riotous! Billy and I were so happy to be together again. He had a separate dressing room. I took everything I needed to start cooking the food. I remember The Jimmy Castor Bunch and Ben E. King had performances before The Spinners. They couldn't finish their bows after their performance because the aroma from the food cooking was wafting out to the stage. Jimmy told the audience that he was sorry, but he smelled home-cooking calling his name.

After the show, someone suggested we all go to Scotland to catch Johnny Ray, who sang one of my favorites, "The Little White Cloud That Cried." We had a chance to talk with him after his show. He was pleasantly surprised to see us and greeted us with joy.

Regretfully, this British adventure had come to an end, and it was time to return home to the states. I had mixed emotions because I was longing to see my children and the rest of my family and friends. I could hardly wait to share my first overseas experience with them.

On the other hand, I wanted more of England and Scotland. There would be several trips to London, England, one of the most memorable trips was sort of a disaster.

The Spinners got ready for a gig, and I didn't want to go. Billy and I got into an argument. I had been shopping and running around all day while he slept, as I always did. I was too tired and didn't want to see the show that night. I just wanted to chill. The chauffer, a different one than the usual guy, drove me to the shops and decided to have a conversation with Billy about how much I purchased. I felt that it was none of the chauffer's business because it wasn't! Billy and I began to argue, not only about my purchases, but the chauffer being all in our personal affairs. Suddenly I began to realize that I did not travel this far to be upset about something so trivial. I was on Billy's job. I decided that the fun was over, and it was time for me to go home. I found Fred, The Spinners' road manager, light man, and had him book me a flight back to the states. He found a flight going to New York on Air Iran. That was perfect for me. I packed my things and took another limo to the airport. I refused the chauffer Billy suddenly befriended.

I arrived in New York at night. I decided to call the chauffer who had driven us every time we visited New York. He was the driver for many stars. His name was Claude Le Mete, and he was the driver for many stars. Claude picked me up at the airport. I explained that I was tired and hungry. He took me to a place where most drivers dined. I then called my friend, Barbara Harris, and she invited me to stay with her for as long as I wanted. The next day I decided to call Marty Lawrence, the vocal coach The Spinners had been using for a few lessons. I also called Noreen, Ahmet Ertegun's (president of Atlantic Records) secretary and arranged to have lunch with her. We went to the famous Sardis. It was obvious that I did not intend to go back to Detroit any time soon. Barbara introduced me to Freddie Murphy, a reporter for *Jet* magazine, a Johnson's publication. He wrote an article on my New York escapades, how I took vocal lessons and shopped at all the high-end stores, getting hats made. I decided to wait until Billy came back from Europe and fly back to Detroit with him.

When we arrived back home, the pace seemed to pick up for The Spinners. They were really in demand. Television shows and gigs were numerous. *Midnight Special*, one of the biggest television shows for hot recording artists, was requesting they come and perform. You can see them in commercials selling old school music

After a few trips to Europe, Philippe, the lead singer, decided to take a break. He wanted the group to be Philippe Wynn and The Spinners. It was a common thing in the business that happens when the lead singer feels they are a big enough to draw on their own. The Spinners voted against the name change. Billy began to look for a replacement for Philippe in case he decided to leave the group and go out on his own.

Billy had a girls' group and booked them in a club in Detroit. He had to go out of town on a gig himself, so I was to oversee things that evening. The group was the opening act for a guy named John Edwards. His band was late getting to the club and John went on and sang, "Danny Boy" without any music. I was very impressed. I later went backstage and introduced myself to him and told him that The Spinners might be looking for a new lead singer. He gave me his contact information. When I told Billy how terrific John was, he and Bobby went to see him perform. John sounded like a mixture of Sam Cooke and Marvin Gaye. Billy and Bobby liked what they heard. When Philippe decided to take a break, John was contacted and agreed to become the lead for The Spinners. Billy had rehearsals for John at our house until all hours of the night. Billy taught John all of the lead parts of their music and started some choreography. Our son, Chucky, taught John the choreography for The Spinners show. When Billy said The Spinners came first, he meant it.

'Billy' Henderson Lionized
At Delightful Surprise Fete

By MARIE TEASLEY

Aren't parties sensational when they honor sensational people? This whole sensational thing got underway at Crajar's Pickwick House on Thursday evening when popular William "Billy" Henderson got the surprise of his life.

Try surprising the handsome singer of Atlantic Records' top chart group? No way, any member of the famed Spinners would tell you. But Billy's ever-popular wife, petite Barbara Henderson, pulled the magic trick and brought out all the entertainment folks to sip, wine and dine on the appointed evening.

"Billie", as he is affectionately called by his fans and peers, found himself in the midst of happy birthday cheers, hundreds of guests and many of his friends from the entertainment fields. Dapper as usual, the honoree wore a steel grey gabardine suit fashioned in raw silk with matching tie and accessories.

Mr. and Mrs. W. B. Henderson

Hostess Barbara, regally gowned for the occasion, chose an Ebony Fashion Fair original; a sheer black silk crepé, floor-length gown fashioned in gold and silver metallic rounds, cut to the waistline at back with provocative slits in the flowing skirt. Adding some European elegance to her fashionable attire, she arrived in a black sable cape, accented with glamorous headwrap that matched her gown.

The lavish decor of the party room left nothing to be desired in the hundreds of floral gifts that arrived from stars and friends in the entertainment business; a unique clown floral figure from Aretha Franklin, apricot-colored roses arrived from Cecil Franklin and wife a sheet cake decorated in musical notes from Atlantic Records, in addition to diamond cuff links, and orchid corsages from Brazelton's Florists.

Henry Watkins, the mixologist, turned out perfect concoctions for the never-ending partymakers who danced to the music of Duncan Sound Company.

Highlighting the sedate atmosphere, the table and dance floor fun, was the impromptu fashion show dedicated to the honoree. "Moses" opened the talent presentations with his own renditions, followed by Barbara's (the honoree's wife) modern dance skit...She brought the house down with applause. Continuing the merriment, the "Henderson Group" performed to a standing ovation. Proud especially of their talents were Mr. and Mrs. Henderson, whose two sons are members of the group.

Lorraine Rudolph, well known artist from Philly, flew in to attend the party and rendered a sensational version of "Happy Birthday, Billy." Cheers went up for "The Powerful Source," a new group being managed by Billy.

Joining in the gift-opening time were Mayor and Mrs. Boo Blackwell, Henry Allen,

vice president of Atlantic Records, Barry Hankerson, Eddie Holland, Dr. and Mrs. Frank Middleman, Dr. Paul Keller, Sherre Jamros, Delores King, Delores Kidwell, Dorothy Lewis, Mr. and Mrs. Versell Ford, Joyce Parrish, John Wilkins, Goodie Goodson, Terry Millinder, Linda Ethridge, Hosana Ethridge, Mr. and Mrs. Lawrence Smith, Mr. and Mrs. Arthur Davison, Patricia White, Edna Henderson, Everett Henderson, Angela Parties, Rudy Smith, Lauren Johnson, Carolyn Lee, Curtis Binner, James Walker, Mr. and Mrs. Robert Mack, Willie Pulliam, Deborah Gordon, Anne Ford, Bobby Smith, Johnny Bradley, the Harold Montgomerys, Gordon Jones, Ernestine Riordiens, Emanuel Butler of Philadelphia, Rita Griffin, Chronicle; Mr. and Mrs. Gene Edwards, Robert Peoples, and many others.

The gifts were opened for a period of several hours, and they were just too fantastic to mention. We'll say no more, the party was sensational.

57

THE SPINNERS

Buddy Allen Management, Inc.
85 West 55th Street, Suite 6C
New York, N. Y. 10019
LT 1-8988-9

apa
AGENCY FOR   THE PERFORMING ARTS,INC
NEW YORK   BEVERLY HILLS

To Hal et Kedra
Enjoy Barbara H's
book
and my portrait

Barbara Purdy

Changes took place, and within them, the family began to play a greater role to The Spinners. Chucky grew up and was a young man with skills even he wasn't aware of. We came from a talented family. I remember when he was about four years old, my sister taught him how to dance. She put his feet on top of hers, and they would dance. Billy's travels kept him busy. He did not notice that his sons were becoming young men and quite talented. Sterling played the piano, danced, and sang. Joe had an ability to quietly handle The Spinners in their dressing rooms. This was one of the most difficult tasks of all when touring due to their different personalities and egos.

Charlie Atkins of Cole & Atkins, a dance duo, was the choreographer for a lot of groups at Motown. He choreographed for The Spinners until he and his wife moved to Las Vegas. The Spinners, needing a new choreographer, hired a dance teacher from Yvonne Johnson's (Baby Jane) dance school. I mentioned to Billy that they should try Chucky out. His remark to me was, "Chucky can't dance."

I talked him into giving Chuck a try. Chuck studied the group and knew their personalities and moves. He became their choreographer (and at one time, road manager) and remained so for more than twenty years until Billy's death. Although it was quite a while before Philippe left, Billy already made it so that John stepped right in for a smooth transition, and the shows continued.

The Spinners needed a reliable valet. They tried several people. I suggested they try Joe, our youngest son. Again, Billy didn't know his potential, but he was willing to give Joe a try. After teaching Joe the basics, Joe was excellent in his capacity as valet and backstage manager until a few years after Billy's death.

Yes, my favorite skating partner kept his word. I traveled with him quite a bit. We went to Atlantic City for them to do some shows at Caesar's Palace. One night after their show, Billy wanted to go to an after-hours club named Club Harlem. It didn't start jumping until after four o'clock in the morning. I was told this was a late-night hangout for the night people, such as pimps and their whores. I had never seen any place like it, so I wanted to go. I never witnessed such a collection of clothing. The outfits ranged from super classy to super flashy. It seemed that the competition for outdressing one another was the golden rule. Billy and I danced and saw a fabulous stage show. Dancing was one of my favorite things to do with Billy. Most couples that I knew didn't have that in common.

In another smaller room, there was a group of four pretty, young girls performing. They could sing their hearts out. They were sisters being managed by their mother, Flo Sledge. The group was called Sister Sledge. They were still in high school. We were all very impressed with their display of tremendous talent. Buddy Allen soon managed and booked the girls with The Spinners. In fact, Chuck and Sterling took two of the Sledge girls to their proms for their high school graduation.

The Spinners' popularity grew faster than we could comprehend. This is what they worked so hard and waited for. We could never imagine to what degree their fame would reach. Not only was there a change in popularity for them, but the demand to associate with them was overwhelming. We had to really make an effort now to find some alone time. I became more interested in the things Billy liked, such as playing golf. He was a caddy almost all of his childhood. It was his way of earning spending money when he was younger.

In his off time, this was his passion, so I barely saw him. He found someone to teach me how to play golf so we could be together. I took lessons from Ben Davis, who worked at Rackham Golf Course. He was a very patient, good instructor. I soon played the game. I wound up loving to play golf. At first, I felt like it was a busman's holiday, you know, driving for your vacation. I worked on my feet all day, so I didn't want to walk around chasing a little white ball. Billy, of course, told me once I learned to play, I would be hooked. He was right. What he didn't tell me that I would still be, as they say, a golf widow. He played with Marvin Gaye, Smokey Robinson, Harvey Fuqua, and several other famous personalities from Motown. They wagered so much per hole. I wanted to go to meet these people. The rest of The Spinners didn't golf.

Billy was a very giving person, as I said earlier. He bought me presents and gave them to me when I picked him up from the airport. The Spinners asked him to stop with the presents because they didn't have anything for their wives. They teased him and called him henpecked because he liked to see me happy.

Soon Billy began inviting whoever was performing in town that he knew to dinner. Cooking was one of my favorite things to do. He loved my cooking and was a very good cook himself. He invited Ronnie Dyson, who was in the movie *Hair* and sang the song "Why Can't I Touch You?" and his mother over after a show. Before I knew it, this became a regular happening. We began to have parties so often the neighbors wanted to come over just to see who came next. This occurrence started snowballing! Billy would invite people and not tell me until the last moment or that day. One day he invited Don Cornelius of *Soul Train* and The Sylvers (*Boogie Fever*), of which there were nine members, all family. I started calling my sister Delores and she would have me pick up whatever she cooked for her family that day. She and I both were what you would call "scratch" cooks, meaning there was no boxed and seldom any canned ingredients. We made lemonade from real lemons and not the concentrate. Delores made the best peach and blackberry cobblers among other foods. Thank you, sis!

I remember Fred, The Spinners' light man, and road manager, said he could marry Delores just for her cobblers. Then there was the time that I called my sister Joyce one night and asked her about having Hugh Masekala (whose hit record at the time was *Grazing in the Grass*) and his band over with our family for Thanksgiving dinner at her house. She said that they could come over the next day, which was Thanksgiving. They were playing a gig at Baker's Keyboard Lounge later that night.

When they arrived at Joyce's house, she had forgotten to tell her husband, Donald. He was letting the guests in, and suddenly these strange men from Africa came in, barely speaking English. He called my sister and asked her, "What in the world is going on?"

Joyce proceeded to explain to him her conversation with me the night before. He laughed and introduced himself and told them to make themselves comfortable. The menu was roast turkey and cornbread dressing, macaroni and cheese, Chitterlings, greens, fruit ambrosia, salad, candied yams with marshmallows on top, green beans, ham, hot dinner rolls, and Mama's sweet-potato pies. They tore into that food as if there was no tomorrow. My mother asked me, "When was the last time they had eaten? When they were in Africa?" We all laughed. It didn't stop the band at all. They kept right on eating like it was going out of style.

They couldn't stay long because they had a show to do later that night. They asked everyone to come and see them. Some of us went to see them perform, but they weren't at the club. The owner made an announcement that they overslept and would be a little late. When they finally arrived, Hugh made their excuses, blaming everything on Mama's sweet-potato pies. American hospitality is nothing to play with. Thank you, family! What would I have done without you?

Billy wasn't in town that Thanksgiving. He performed elsewhere. Due to his schedule, he was seldom home for our anniversary, which was the twenty-sixth of November. Since our anniversary was on the same day, Pervis's wife, Claudreen, and I decided we would celebrate together! It became a sort of tradition for us.

Eventually, trying to cook for the who's who in entertainment became too much! I finally drew the line when I found myself barbequing in the snow with boots on. We had a gas grill, which made it somewhat easier. Hugh Masekala was back in the States from Africa for an event and, since Billy was in town, dropped in hungry and grinning. It was an honor to cook for him, yes, but looking like an Eskimo barbecuing in the snow wasn't going to cut it.

Food continued to play a part in our memorable relationship. Billy brought food home on some of his trips. I remember that he loved a place in Chicago named Ribs and Bibs. He picked up some ribs after a show and had them packed with the sauce on them. As he came through the airport, security decided to search his luggage. An agent put his hand in the package with the barbecue sauce and drew it out, loaded with sauce. He looked at Billy. Billy was saying to himself, "You better not wipe your hand on my stuff," and he glared back at the agent. Finally, the agent had to leave his post to wash his hand. This did Billy all the good in the world. The ribs got through but were not enjoyed due to the incident. He would recall and laugh at this unpleasant event for years to come. The hustler in him relished getting over on people.

Life at that time was pleasant as well as exhilarating. I began to get involved in a lot of activities when I wasn't on the road with Billy. I had a friend named Janet Howard Washington, who worked for a Michigan State Representative and lived very close by. Janet was politically involved in quite a few exciting projects. She was very astute in her capacity. It was through Janet that I became involved in the campaign to reelect Coleman Young as mayor of Detroit for a second term. Coleman went to high school in Detroit with my father. He was also one of the first black bombardiers in the Tuskegee Airmen. Coleman was a very handsome, strong-willed, self-assured, not-married-at-the-time man. Every woman in Detroit, it seemed, had high hopes to be Mrs. Coleman Young.

Janet was excellent at networking. I already met Jackie Vaughn, Janet's boss, at an earlier time, so I was thrilled when we became reacquainted. And so came another exciting phase of my life.

I remember there was a benefit dinner for Coleman's campaign one evening at Cobo Hall Convention Center. Janet and I attended. We were seated with the some of the most influential people in Detroit. After my trips to London, where I was treated with such honor and care, it suddenly occurred to me that all these important people were just people, as human as anyone else you could find. Each had their respective quirks and issues, just as I had my own. I realized that I didn't have to be perfect to belong, I just had to claim my right to be among them.

There would be several functions held at the Manoogian Mansion, the Mayor of Detroit's home. It is a fitting home for a mayor. It is situated off the Detroit River, complete with an impressive boat house.

You could only attend these functions by invitation only, which meant that your name had to be on the guest list. I tried to get Billy to attend some of the activities with me, but he always had something else to do that was more important to him. I remember I was at one such affair when there was a commotion at the front door. I looked up, and it was Billy. I heard him saying I invited him to attend with me, and he was late. Coleman's head of security told him that he was sorry, but Billy's name was not on the guest list. Billy replied with, "But I see her car parked right out front." The security said how sorry he was; he really couldn't let Billy in because his name was not on the list. I asked Billy earlier about attending. He again refused to go with me, citing something else of more importance. Therefore, he was not put on the list. When I returned home, Billy was a little angry about the incident at the mayor's home. He thought because he was one of The Spinners, he did not have to be on a guest list; he could just say who he was, and that was his ticket anywhere.

This was the beginning of many occasions whereby I would be in the presence of the mayor, and Billy wouldn't. There was a wedding at the mayor's mansion. We were invited, and all of the wives of The Spinners showed up. (The guys were away on a gig.) Claudia Young, Coleman's niece was the beautiful bride with her handsome husband, Freddy. It was a gala affair. Claudia and I became and still are cherished friends.

International travel beckoned. The Spinners were booked overseas again. This time, they were to go to London, England, Paris, France, and Munich, Germany. Billy asked me to go. Of course, my answer was yes with a capital Y. Philippe was still with the group at this point, anticipating his departure from the group. If I remember correctly, he served in the armed forces in Germany.

We flew to London, England, first. We spent a few wonderful days there. We went again to Chelsea to the restaurant, Chelsea's Rendezvous. We had our usual dishes of the most delectable food

I have ever tasted, including Billy's favorite, Peking duck. Peking duck was a duck that had been pumped with air between the skin of the duck and the flesh. It would hang for at least twenty-four hours before cooking. (I remember preparing a duck while living with my mother. She came home from work and proceeded to wash her work uniform and found a duck, hanging in the basement with a fan blowing on it I had fun explaining that one.) Once you cooked it, the skin of the duck was very crispy because while it was hanging, you brushed it with a honey-based solution. The end results were to eat the duck on a pancake-type crepe called a "doily." On this doily, you would place pieces of the duck meat, strips of the crispy skin, topped with strips of cucumbers and scallions, and finish with plum sauce, then wrap somewhat like an enchilada. Eating was an experience in itself. Now you know why this was one of Billy's favorite dishes.

We soon left London and flew Air France to the Charles DeGaulle Airport in Paris. I remember Buddy Allen making the remark that I had more luggage than The Spinners. We laughed about it! We drank Mimosas (champagne mixed with orange juice) and ate Brie (a soft, tasty cheese) on the flight over to Paris. It was about ten o'clock in the morning. Since I was on another escapade, I indulged myself.

I never thought that going through an airport could be so delightful. We suddenly were in futuristic-type surroundings. Escalators enclosed in huge glass tubes opened up to the baggage claim. It was exhilarating!

Billy wanted to go to the hotel and rest before the show. I pointed out to him that this was a once-in-a-lifetime opportunity, and I wanted to see Paris. He consented. We took a taxi, which was a Mercedes Benz, to the Eiffel Tower. My toes tingled as the elevator went to the top. We viewed the splendor of the city, including Notre Dame. (The driver spoke only French and Portuguese. I took four years of French in high school, so I had him go to a bookstore to pick up a French-English dictionary). We took movies of me dancing with my black-diamond, mink hat, muff and coat on, at the top of the Eiffel Tower.

It swayed, but we were told that it was constructed to sway with the wind, or else it would break. Americans pronounced it as the "Eyeful Tower," while the French pronounce it as "*Eé*ful Tower." As we descended, we noticed a restaurant and decided to have lunch in the Eifel Tower. Now I know why the French are famous for their sauces. We both planned on having some kind of fish dish. When the dishes came, we looked at each other because the fish seemed rather bland-looking, but when we added the sauce, salad, and the bread, I can't begin to describe the taste! Scrumptious would not even begin to be adequate. After such an exquisite lunch, we decided to take a brief tour of Paris. The driver took us to the Arch de Triumph and the river, Seine. Billy wanted to know where we could buy some Joy perfume. I managed to ask the driver, and he took us to the *rue* (street) of perfumes.

Billy introduced me to Joy, the costliest perfume in the world, early in our relationship. It was his favorite, so when we came upon some in a perfume shop in Paris, we were like one-eyed dogs in a sausage factory. I tried on a perfume called Cabochard because Billy said it had a sensuous smell. Then there was a heavenly fragrance just for furs named Revillion; without your fur on, it had no particular smell. Once I put on my fur, it was beyond words! I fell in love with all of the fragrances.

The sales lady introduced me to a fragrance that was Liz Taylor's favorite at the time. It is named Fracas. I can still find every fragrance with the exception of Revillion. I still wear them all, according to whatever the occasion calls for. Billy was a nut for sweet-smelling fragrances. In fact, he saturated himself in men's colognes so much you could always tell when he was in a room by the scent he left behind. I remember Marvin Gaye, among other stars, would ask Billy what scent was he wearing, and he would smile. Sometimes he told them, and sometimes he didn't. I always brought him something back I thought he would like in a scent from wherever I went.

The French-English dictionary came in handy for everyone. The next morning, I interpreted for the rest of The Spinners when they were ready to order breakfast. They performed that evening and were all invited to a bordello, a place of prostitution. I asked Billy what it was like, and he gave me some vague nonsense of an answer. I ignored the subject and continued to enjoy my time in France.

Billy and I made a sort of pact that there would be no other women or problems when I was out on the road with him. The State of Michigan was off-limits and especially Detroit; this was where our home was. He was to bring home just himself and his money. Hallelujah, these were pre-AIDS times. This was in the early seventies.

The next leg of our journey was taking a flight to Germany on Lufthansa Airlines. The atmosphere as we boarded the plane was very cold and somewhat hostile. The stewardesses were not very receptive, seeing all these people of color with a Jewish couple. Sister Sledge and their mother were also with us. Suddenly I don't know how everyone else felt, but I wasn't so anxious to go to Germany anymore.

When we arrived at the airport in Germany, there was an uneventful reception. I did not feel comfortable in the least. On our way to Munich, we saw a convoy of American-Army soldiers. We waved to them as we passed. When we got to the hotel, we received the same cool reception that we encountered on the plane and airport. It was very apparent that we weren't welcome. Buddy and Connee wanted to see Dachau, the place where the concentration camp was. It is a museum now. This was the most depressing expression of man's inhumanity to man as far as I was concerned. It was inconceivable and very hard for the heart and mind to digest that such events could have happened, and there was proof still in existence as a reminder. Ironically, Germany was aesthetically one of the most picturesque countries I had ever seen. I had no desire to take pictures and was glad that it was to be a short stay. The performance was well received because by then, The Spinners' music had become universal!

Then I received a compliment worth the Germany trip. Flo Sledge said to me, "I can see why Billy brings you with him. You bring home to him out here on the road." Happily we left to return to the United States. More than ever I began to appreciate my homeland, flaws and all. This incident made me aware of the highs and lows of being a public figure and how it is not always glamour and excitement. You have to have a certain constitution to fit into certain roles in life. I have never felt so helpless and out of control as when I was in Germany. It weighed heavily on the soul!

After arriving back in the States and, finally, in Detroit, I felt my confidence return, as I found a social scene now abuzz from Aretha Franklin having some magnificent parties. My, my, my, I still have one of the invitations; it was the most elegant invitation I ever received. It must have cost a pretty penny.

I remember one party in particular. We arrived at her beautiful home, and a driver complete in a red coat, tails and top hat on picked us up at our car and drove us in a horse-driven carriage to her door. Aretha greeted us with a lei of baby orchids. She was having a luau. The white sand on her lawn was so deep you had to remove your high-heel shoes. In fact, Aretha said to me, "You have to take your shoes off, Miss Thing."

There was roasted, suckling pig with an apple in its mouth, with all the trimmings, the most expensive caviar, and baby lamb chops being served on platters by servers. Word is that by the very next day, there wasn't a grain of sand left on her lawn. It had all been vacuumed up.

I met a lot of celebrities at her parties: "Magic" Johnson and Clifton Davis, to name a few. I could fill this book with names of the most fascinating people that I came to know.

Aretha loved to cook, so Billy and I had a barbecue pit made for her with her initials and music notes on it. Quite some time later, she said to Billy, "Henderson, you know, I wore that pit out." Billy smiled with pride. He liked giving things that pleased people.

I also met a wonderful photographer named Linda Solomon. She photographed Muhammad Ali, Candice Bergen, Mickey Rooney, Sammy Davis Jr., and Mikhail Baryshnikov, to name a few. Linda and her family still remain very close friends.

The Spinners were booked with a host of artists to perform in Zaire, Africa in 1974. There was to be a fight with Muhammad Ali and George Foreman. There also was to be a festival surrounding the historic event. The roster of artists consisted of personalities such as The Pointer Sisters, Sister Sledge, Johnny Pacheco, B.B. King, James Brown, Etta James, Bill Withers, Hugh Masekala, Lloyd Price,

Miriam Makeba (an African singer who sang with a clicking sound). You would expect Aretha Franklin, The Queen of Soul, to be in such a lineup, wouldn't you? Billy said Aretha Franklin wouldn't go because if the airplane were to crash, or something were to happen, the loss would be too great because too many famous artists were on one airplane!

I wanted to go, but Billy said that they would be on a chartered plane, and no one could come except the ones listed on the roster. I went to get his passport updated and told the man to do mine also. I made up my mind that I would be going to Africa.

Billy flew me to New York the night before they were to leave for Africa. The Spinners had a Madison-Square performance that night. Afterward, while we were in the limousine, Billy gave me a black Russian, sable cape and the most beautiful black evening gown costing $1500 at the least! I was overwhelmed. As I ran my fingers along the Sable, I realized that the gifts were to pacify me into dropping the idea of traveling to Zaire. I packed my new possessions and told him I still wanted to go. He still said no.

The next morning, I flew back to Detroit highly disappointed. After all, Africa is the motherland to our people. And talk about history! I read so much about the history and wanted to experience the continent for myself.

Billy called me later to let me know when they would be leaving, promising to call when he arrived in Zaire. He called and told me of trouble they had on the airplane. James Brown insisted on bringing his piano. Billy said that everybody on board had to shift to one end of the plane so that the plane could take off. I sympathized somewhat. I wanted to travel to Zaire!

Strangely enough, Billy wasn't there for more than two days when he called and asked me to fly there. I was thrilled. Hugh Masekala made arrangements through the African Embassy for me to have my immunization shots where the pilots took theirs at Kennedy Airport in New York. I suppose the barbecue I cooked back then paid off.

My mother began to fret about me flying so far alone. I assured her that I would be fine. In fact, I was half packed because I somehow knew that I would be going. I left for New York the very next morning and arrived at Kennedy Airport, and they had everything ready for me. I was ushered into the room where the pilots were inoculated and was warned that the process should have been done, at the minimum, a week prior to my flight. I was given my shots quickly with a warning that I might have a reaction.

I went to the gate elated and boarded a flight going to Paris. By the time I finished immigration, I was exhausted and hungry. I began to feel a little queasy, so I decided to take a nap until it was time for the dinner. I just finished my meal when suddenly there was a terrific drop in altitude. My tray that held my food jumped. The stewardess came and told everyone to put on their seatbelts on. My gut wrenched. Some of the passengers groaned and gasped. My feet went sweaty and cold. *I couldn't help but to hear Aretha Franklin singing* Chain of Fools *in my mind. Who wouldn't try to travel to Africa if they had a chance? Who wouldn't want to be there for such a historical moment? I gripped my armrests and imagined my things floating about in the ocean. Would I be pulled out of the ocean by some crane like Otis Redding? I started to prepare for the worst-case scenario. The dip and sputters seemed like hours, as if set on draining everyone in the plane out of their composure before the inevitable. But then, suddenly with a final drop, we hit smooth skies.* We survived!

We arrived in Paris and had to change planes. There was only about an hour in between flights. Still rattled from the flight, I thought of something to calm my nerves. That's right, I went to the gift shop, bought a few things, went to the next gate, and waited for the next flight.

The next flight took us to the Nice, France. We had a three-hour layover, so I took a taxi to the Cote d'Azur, known in English as the French Riviera. The French Rivera is the Mediterranean coastline of the southeastern corner of France. It is known as the playground and vacation spot of the British, Russians, and aristocrats such as Queen Victoria and King Edward VII. I had to see it, being so close!

I walked around and went to a restaurant to have a snack. The French Riviera was one of the most picturesque places I have ever been to. I am glad that I satisfied that curiosity. By the way. the maître d at the restaurant and the waiter both were two of the most handsome men I have ever seen with the exception of some movie stars. The flight to get there seemed a bit more tolerable, with the eye candy being so memorable.

I boarded the flight from Nice, France, to Johannesburg, South Africa. During the flight, we flew from daylight into darkness. The pilot informed us we just crossed the international date line. It was eerie yet delightful! At Johannesburg, we had few hours' layover, but I was not so adventurous. I remained at the airport because I was in South Africa, the heart of apartheid. I didn't want any racial confrontations. Germany was still too fresh on the mind.

After about thirteen hours, I finally arrived at the Zaire airport. Problems arose from the start because of the timing of my inoculation. I was refused entry into the country. It made little difference to me. I decided someone was going to let me in. I waited and looked for Billy to meet me. No Billy! I asked if anyone knew where The Spinners were staying. When I said Spinners, they let me go through customs.

I got a taxi to where The Spinners were staying, and I found the prince of Detroit still sleeping. By this time, I was so angry I could barely speak. I got past the anger and wanted to know why he would ask me to come and not meet me at the airport. His excuse was that he just overslept. It was a weak reason, but I didn't travel all that way to be angry and upset. I unpacked with a lot of noise, snatching of clothes, eventually settling. Later we went to dinner, and when we returned, I noticed a giant mosquito in our room. I refused to go to bed until Billy got rid of it. He finally shooed it out of our room. I got under the mosquito net and didn't come out until the next morning. I learned that one of the other Spinners got bitten and contracted malaria.

We had a driver and an interpreter, so I decided to go to the Ivory Market by way of the interpreter's suggestion. I didn't know what the Ivory Market entailed, but I was willing to find out. I went and ran into the Sister Sledge. It was an outdoor market, with everything from ivory pieces to malachite jewelry. I found out rather quickly that you could trade Polaroid pictures for different items.

Upon returning to the villa, the interpreter told Billy, "She no need me. She do fine." I told them I understood money and bartering no matter what the language. I traded pictures for all colors of amber jewelry, a petrified sap from certain trees. I found out that the natives liked to see themselves appear on the pictures. I even got red amber, which is very rare. Malachite is the ore that copper comes from. I bartered pictures for a complete set of malachite: earrings, bracelet, and a necklace. Ivory was not illegal then, so I traded pictures for ivory bracelets. I had a very fruitful day.

The next day we were invited to Muhammad Ali's training camp for lunch. The ride out to the camp was hilarious! The driver and the interpreter arrived to take us. They were impeccably dressed, so starched and well fitted.

We all piled into the cars and drove off. Slowly everyone looked at each other, and their noses were turned up, as if they smelled something foul. Everyone checked themselves to make sure they put on their deodorant. The driver put his arm on the window, and suddenly everyone realized that it was the driver and the interpreter. They were clean, but deodorant was a western custom. They did not know anything about masking their natural scents. Boy, did we ever get our fair share of smelling their armpits! The Spinners complained and offered them some deodorant. They looked at us as if they couldn't understand why we of all people wore deodorant.

We finally came to the entrance of a game preserve, which was where Mobutu's summer home was located off the Belgian Congo River. The drive to the house was fascinating because giraffes, ostriches, and all sort of animals roamed free. The distance was approximately ten miles or more from the entrance to the house. Mobutu was the president of Zaire. He let Muhammad Ali and his entourage stay there. Ali had his training camp set up on the premises.

Lunch was delectable! Ali's mother was the head chef. We were all seated at one long table. After lunch, Ali sat around with us and talked. He looked at me and asked who I was. (He was quite a womanizer.) Billy spoke up quickly and said to him, "You've been in the ring with professionals. You never had to fight a short, fat, out-of-shape, alley apple-throwing cat! Man, stay away from her. She's my wife, and I don't fight fair."

Everyone howled with laughter! I later asked Billy what an alley apple was. He looked at me and asked, "You never heard that expression before? It is a huge rock from the alley."

After a while, Ali decided to do some training. There were a few members of the press waiting to interview him and take a few pictures. Philippe of The Spinners mentioned that he competed in the Golden Gloves (amateur boxing) at one time. Ali challenged Philippe to spar with him one round, with the rest of The Spinners as Philippe's second. Philippe accepted. I don't remember Philippe lasting more than a few minutes, if not seconds.

Later that evening we had to leave to go back because the concert was going to be in the big arena that night. The artists on the bill that day were Sister Sledge, The Spinners, and James Brown. They all went back to get dressed in their dressing rooms. Sister Sledge opened first, then The Spinners opened up with a rousing performance, under unique conditions. Billy commented later, "Yeah, they built a stadium to hold eighty-five thousand people with four bathrooms. Talk about poor plumbing."

Plumbing was the last thing on the mind right before the performance. The Spinners were used to coming off the stage and greeting the audience, but this time, the audience greeted *them*. Some of them got onstage and pulled at their ties, at their bracelets, or whatever they wore, their jewelry, looking for souvenirs. The Spinners later admitted to being a little frightened by the onslaught. I rushed past them, trying not to be knocked over by so many people. That pressure of people crushing against you, it became hard to breathe.

Throngs of them rushed in, speaking French. The Spinners only spoke English. I spoke very little French, so panic spread. I had never seen so many people coming toward me without being able to communicate. I thought of The Beatles and other groups that dealt with such frenzy. I decided that it was not the time for me to be in the middle of the chaos, so I got on the bus with the bus driver.

Billy eventually made it to the bus. He laughed and said that he looked everywhere for me. I told him that I thought it was safer to stay back on the bus because I knew the bus was going back to the compound of villas, where it was safe. After The Spinners opened the show, there was a short intermission. James Brown was set to perform next.

Everyone waited for James Brown to appear. His musical conductor, Maceo, played the introduction. The singers and dancers came out. But there was no James Brown. Everyone kept waiting, and finally after the fifth introduction, maybe closer to the seventh or eighth introduction, James finally came out, and the crowd went wild. They went crazy! They were so glad to see James, but the problem was that half of the people already left the stadium because they weren't used to staying up at that hour, and especially to see somebody that they hadn't seen before. The Godfather of Soul delivered a show-stopping performance. It turned out to be quite a night.

The next day I met The Pointer Sisters and Etta James. It had been a while since I was in a place where there were so many famous acts gathered at the same time, at the same place, for the same cause. There were acts scheduled for each night of the ten-day festival. It was supposed to be a festival celebrating the fight, but the crowd was all for Ali. Every time Ali walked by, they hollered, "Ali muumbayaa," which meant, "Ali, kill him."

I remember when Foreman would come around they would boo him. To his detriment, Foreman kept German-shepherd dogs around him wherever he went. The pets were the same breed as police used to control crowds. George wasn't aware that he set himself up for that and lost the contest of winning the people over to his side.

While George went on to lose the fight inside the ring as well, others got quite comfortable. Someone discovered some marijuana, which was called African gun-gee. You could apparently buy it for ten dollars a pound. It was very, very cheap, and so the party was on. Everybody enjoyed themselves in Africa, but soon it came time to return back to the States. There were a few people who were going to stay there, and there were some who were going to return, so I didn't have to worry about catching a flight back by myself. They told me that I was invited to fly back with Billy. That was wonderful because I got a chance to meet Lloyd Price's mother-in-law, which was Qwanda's mother, his wife at the time. We had a wonderful time. She and I were on the plane having a conversation, and all of a sudden we smell this smell, and we see Billy walking up and down the aisle with incense. Everybody who had gotten some of the African gun-gee, decided to light up. Talk about flying high. Mom looked at me, and I looked at her, and I said, "Well, Mom, there is nothing else to do. Let's go to sleep." So we both decided to curl up and go to sleep. The next thing we knew, the plane landed in Spain, and it was at an hour when everything was closed.

We went through Spain's airport, and everything was shut down. After they refueled, we were off to New York. As we approached the airport in New York, the pilot got on the loud speaker and told everybody, "I don't know what you're going to do with it—smoke it, eat it, chew it, or whatever—but we are going into customs, and you have to get rid of whatever you have."

You should have seen the scramble. They lit up and smoked as much as they could, and those that couldn't smoke ended up flushing it. The pilot circled the airport until he couldn't circle anymore, and finally we had to land, red-eyed, light-headed, and so very mellow.

When we got to customs, there were so many people on that airplane customs took one look at us and passed us all on through without looking through any bags. Those who bought the "smoke" were angry because they could have brought it through with them; but honestly, they wouldn't dare have taken the chance. Africa, and all that the trip encompassed, was an experience one would never forget.

Returning to so-called normal life proved to be somewhat boring, but that changed soon enough. We were only home about a month, when Billy's younger cousin came by and said that he was rehearsing to be in a play. He asked me to try out because he was having such fun. I was looking for something to do, so I decided to check things out. Every major part was taken. The play was called *Selma.* I watched the part of Mama Sweets, and I thought that I could do a better job because the part was being played by someone so young they couldn't relate to the part of a seventy-year-old grandmother. I went home and got into character by buying a grey wig and a cane and practicing the part. When the next rehearsal came, I showed up dressed as an elderly grandmother and got the part.

Redd Fox (the comedian) and Tommy Butler collaborated, wrote, and produced the play. It was based on the march to Selma. Martin Luther King, Ralph Abernathy, and Rosa Parks were the principal characters portrayed in the play until Billy talked to Tommy Butler, who made Mama Sweets one of the principal characters. Mama Sweets was the fictionalized grandmother of the three little girls killed when the 16th Street Baptist church was bombed. Ernie Banks, a renowned actor, played the part of Ralph Abernathy. I was thrilled to be in something that he was already a part of!

Billy didn't want me traveling as a cast member only, but as a principal character. He also asked for so much in salary for my part. The play was three of six weeks into rehearsal. Tommy made it clear to me that if I couldn't cut the mustard, so to speak, that I would be up for elimination. We were to go on a three-month tour. The cities we were to perform in included Norfolk, Virginia, Elizabeth City, North Carolina, and finally, Tuskegee, Alabama. Rehearsals were long and grueling, yet exciting. I learned how to get into character and stay, whether I was acting on stage or not.

Finally, the time came for us to start the tour. Billy also made sure of my accommodations when he negotiated my salary. I was so glad he took care of those matters because I knew nothing about what it entailed to be on the road as a performer. His experience at such things was far greater than mine. Hallelujah for that!

I soon had a life-impacting experience while out on the road. The day arrived when we all piled into a bus and headed out for what would turn out to be a truly unforgettable experience. The first night on the bus was one gigantic rush! Anticipation ran high! Nobody slept! When we arrived in Norfolk Virginia, we were in the heart of town and noticed a torn-up wreath, which was placed there in observation of Martin Luther King's birthday. We found out that it was partially destroyed by the Ku Klux Klan, or KKK. We also later found out that the Grand Wizard of the Ku Klux Klan lived in Norfolk. Later Tommy let us know that we wouldn't be performing in Norfolk because he was warned there would be trouble, even though the play *The Wiz* just left town. The sheriff and his deputies in the play were young men with painted white faces. Consequently, we had to perform across the river at an auditorium in the black section of town. We persevered and performed.

On opening night, as we finished the final act and took bows, someone in the cast called me, saying, "They want you, Mama Sweets." Tommy told me to take a bow. I curtsied, and as I straightened up, the audience rose to their feet and began to chant, "Mama Sweets, Mama Sweets." I just stood there and watched them. I was frightened and excited both at the same time. It was then that I realized that you never rehearse the bow.

Some of the people in the audience had worn their bloodstained shirts and other clothing from when the actual event occurred. They were bitten by dogs and beaten by the sheriff back then and his so-called posse. This play, in particular, was very emotional and surreal to them. It portrayed a very important part of history, and they were living reminders of this never-to-be-forgotten event. Their grandchildren and generations to come would be reminded always of these horrific times. My heart both ached and swelled for them

I woke to the fact that the grandmother in the south was not only the matriarch, but the most highly respected member of the southern family. This play was so important to the people it made me reflect on my performance. Could I repeat the same performance with the kind of passion needed for the rest of the tour? What was to be fun and a means of exhilaration became very serious to me. I read about the march to Selma and saw parts of the incident on television.

We were booked to perform in that theater for a week. The house was packed and sold out every night! We got standing ovations every night! We spent almost every night after the play signing autographs. I remember there was a little boy, I guess he was about seven or eight years of age. His dark, shining skin and eyes made my throat thicken with adoration. His mother said he saw the two previous performances and wanted desperately to meet the grandmother. I introduced myself to him, and he began to cry. I asked what the trouble was, and he said, "I want to meet the grandmother, not you!" I had changed to my street clothing. I finally convinced him who

I was by speaking in my stage voice. After that night, I greeted the people while still in costume.

The last night of performing in Norfolk was mixed in feelings for everyone in the cast, it seemed. The anticipation of what awaited in the next town, and the realization that racism was alive and well were both sobering and galvanizing! Most of the cast, if not all of us, were born and raised up north, where racism was mostly hidden by indirect language and phony smiles. We read about the situation in the south, or saw what the news media wanted to be seen in the newspaper and television. But this, to see so barefaced, vile, and unrelenting, brought the sound of the heart up to thrash in the ears.

The director, Tommy, went through similar situations before. We weren't the first cast to perform *Selma* in the south. He knew what to do. He kept everyone calm.

After the final performance, we decided to go out and celebrate by having something to eat. Everyone got dressed up. The only place that was open at that time of night on a Sunday was Burger King. While we were in the Burger King getting our food, there were some young, white men from the Naval Base in Norfolk harassing some of the female dancers. (Tommy wasn't there because he was finalizing his business.) The young men in the cast started to defend the girls because they indicated that they didn't want to be bothered. The Navy guys started to shove our men, and the fight was on.

The young men in the cast had a scene in which they did karate. They began to do some karate moves, and before we knew it, the fight was over. Our guys went away unscathed. They never even mussed their suits. Meanwhile, someone called the police. Tommy arrived there just before the police and was told what happened by the manager of Burger King. The police took the Navy guys away. The police told Tommy that we could press charges. Tommy told them we were leaving that night and wouldn't be around long enough. We all applauded our guys for taking care of business.

We went back to the hotel and packed for the next bus ride to Elizabeth City, North Carolina. I don't remember exactly how long the trip was. I do remember the trip was mostly on two-lane highways and incredibly dark. There were no gas stations or anything with lights along this stretch of road. I recalled reading about lynching taking place along roads such as these. In my mind's eye. I could see the bodies of lynched men hanging from the trees. The rest of the cast must have been thinking something similar, or it seemed that way because those who had not gone to sleep didn't talk at all.

When we finally arrived in Elizabeth City, it was in the very early morning, about five o'clock a.m., and very cold. We were to stay at two hotels. The dancers and the rest of the cast were to stay at one, and the principal cast members were supposed to stay at the other. We came to the one where the majority of the cast was to stay. It was dark and closed down for the night. After a while of making noise, a rather angry, portly white man, who was the owner, came to the door with no shoes and no shirt on. He angrily, in no uncertain terms, reluctantly let the cast members in, while muttering to himself about how late it was. We couldn't go anywhere else. There weren't that many places in that town that could house the amount of people we had in one place, so we remained where we were.

After the cast members settled in, we went to The Holiday Inn, the only well-known hotel they had in town. It was in the dead of winter, January, in fact. We were told that the heat was not on in the rooms that we booked. He said that the heat was scheduled to come on automatically at 7o'clock that morning and not before. So you would have to freeze for about an hour and a half in an unheated room.

The coffee shop in The Holiday Inn was open and heated. Since we had no choice but to wait until 7 a.m., most of the principal actors and Tommy and his wife decided to wait there and have breakfast. I always traveled with an electric blanket, so I wasn't quite in the same fix as everyone else. There was one glitch in my situation: I was paired with a homosexual girl as a roommate. She looked at me with a look of glee, as if we were going to share the blanket. I let her know in no uncertain terms that sharing was not an option. She got the message and decided to go to the coffee shop.

After such a disappointing beginning, we hoped that everything would be better once the performances began. We were so wrong! After a day or so, the rooms at the other hotel were ransacked, and some items were stolen. We reported the theft to the sheriff. It fell on deaf ears because the sheriff was the cousin of the hotel owner.

Suddenly we felt like we were back in time to the days of nepotism, of racist white families, either incompetent or simply spiteful, running small towns unchecked; back to a time when black people wound up missing without so much as a mention in the morning paper. We became closer than ever, never going any place alone. Everyone was careful, cautious, and ever vigilant. Just what would we do if it became necessary?

The sense of disbelief and rage was palpable. This was the eighties, for god's sake! What in heaven's name was happening? Would this hideous side of American culture ever end? Where was the hope for the peace that Martin Luther King had marched, taken beatings, and died for? Would I ever see it in my day? Or were we hoping in vain? I came out on the road to perform in a play about some of the events I read about. I never dreamed that the part that I portrayed would be looked upon as some sort of crusade for a cause that would be never-ending!

The sheriff and or his deputies were always around, especially when we were not performing. They were at every restaurant, every store, and just about every place we decided to go. Finally, the time came when the show came to an end. The girl who portrayed Coretta King and I decided to rent a car and drive to the next town in which we were to perform, even though the director was warned in advance not to show up.

Tommy Butler received another call concerning Selma and the play. He decided that it would be for the best, and everyone's safety, that we go on to Tuskegee University in Tuskegee, Alabama, thereby cancelling our appearance in Selma, Alabama. I recalled having read about the sheriff of Selma with his dogs. He made the dogs attack the people upon his command. I remember how some of the people in the audiences were victims of those dogs and wore their bloodstained clothing to the performances.

The happy-go-lucky atmosphere amidst the cast changed. Everyone just wanted to finish the tour and return home. Most of the cast were young adults with little or no understanding of true racism, not that I was so knowledgeable and experienced on the subject. Being raised up in north was so profoundly different.

The reception at Tuskegee was warm and far less tense. We were able to relax and perform in comfort. Everything went very well. This was the end of the tour. We piled on the bus and were happy to be heading home.

Once we were back in Detroit, I didn't want to stop my acting career. I began to seek out parts that were suited for me. Opening night at the Detroit Repertory Theater, Billy sent me a dozen roses even though he did not attend the play. The kids were happy I was home. They expected Billy to be on the road, but not me. They were young men by then and pretty much on their own, meaning they had their own agendas. Sterling and Chuck got married and were having children.

After a while, the acting parts for me were few and far between. The Spinners, on the other hand, did more television shows, and their records got even more airplay. Their popularity seemed to be endless. They performed on *The Mike Douglas Show*. I really enjoyed that one. Mike told The Spinners that he heard there was a food connoisseur in the group. Everyone laughed and pointed to Billy. He asked Billy where he could find the best Coney Island hotdog. Billy told him about Pink's Coney Island stand in Los Angeles. He was satisfied with the answer and went to a few more questions. When he finally he asked Billy where the best seafood in Cleveland was (the show was being taped there), Billy answered, "Captain Frank's Seafood."

Life was great! I even tried to keep the spice in our lives going. One day I had to pick Billy up from the airport. It was winter. I put on my black mink coat with the hat and muff to match. Billy was happy to see me. I got out of the car to greet him, and the wind blew open the bottom of my coat. Billy's eye got so big. He said to me, "Hurry, get in the car." I didn't have any clothes on beneath all the fur. When we got home, we parked the car and locked ourselves in the house for a couple of days. Fun time! Our time! These were the moments that I looked forward to, shutting out the world, just Billy and me.

The Spinners were asked to go to California to do *The Jerry Lewis Telethon*, which was a huge charitable event that was being televised. Billy asked me if I would like to go with him. I was so thrilled I could hardly tell him yes. I finally got to meet Ida Lupino, a world-famous movie star, Jack Benny, a comedian with his own television show, and of course, Jerry Lewis, a very funny comedian, among many others. I wanted to take pictures with them, but I was too embarrassed to ask. After all, Billy was in the same status as they. Being a wife, I didn't want to make him ashamed of me. No one else there was taking pictures.

Great milestones continued to be realized. The Spinners became the first group in their genre and of Afro-American descent to have a star on the Walk of Fame. They were excited because the only other group with such an honor at the time was The Mills Brothers.

While we were in Los Angeles, Billy and I visited the Farmers Market quite often for fresh juice and the best English (Little John's) toffee I ever tasted. Every time he went to Los Angeles afterward, I could always look for him to bring some back for me.

Things began to change in The Spinners' management. Billy had been screening everybody the group needed to make them fit and ready professionally. I watched and offered my advice when he wanted or needed it. After all, I had been a bookkeeper for the Detroit Board of Education. They were making more money than ever. Billy said that if he made the money that I could help him keep it. One thing he left out was I could keep what I knew about. The change in The Spinners affected our marriage. I learned the real meaning of the old saying, "Money changes things."

Billy started not coming home with the other guys. It seemed strange. I didn't know what the problem was, or if there was a problem. I felt stuck in a situation that I had no control over. My marriage was woven into Spinners matters. With my other marriages, I would know what to do. I now understood better than ever why The Spinners came first. They were like the wife. To Billy, I was the other woman. I tried talking with Billy, not knowing that he was facing a bigger dilemma. The harder I tried, the worse things got. The one thing we realized was that we loved each other. This was scary to both of us.

The Spinners settled whatever was amiss and continued without missing a beat. Things got somewhat better for Billy and me, yet remained a little strained. I couldn't put my finger on the problem. He did something that was more interesting than coming home after gigs.

The Grammy Awards were coming up. I wanted to go, but I wouldn't ask Billy because I found out that if I waited for him to ask or invite me, I would have a much better time. The day of the awards finally came. Billy left that morning to do a gig some place not far from New York. He called me that afternoon and told me that he wanted me there. I called the airline and made reservations. I then packed the dress and accessories that I intended to wear and left. I arrived in New York and took a taxicab to the place. When I arrived, there was no Billy, and the program was about to start. (There were no cell phones back then.) By this time, I was totally frustrated and at a loss as to what I should do. I had an usher find Billy. When I saw him, I took a step toward him and gave him my bag. The usher reminded us of the shortness of time before the program was starting.

Billy was showing me to my seat when the heel of my shoe broke. I was so embarrassed (they were new shoes) I had to chuckle to myself as I hobbled to my seat. I was seated in the second row from the front in the middle section between Andy Williams and Kate Smith, two world-renowned singers. I gave my shoe to the usher and asked him if he could somehow do a temporary fix. He came back and passed the shoe down the row back with a sympathetic nod of no. There I was feeling like Lucy in *I Love Lucy*. All eyes followed the shoe as it was passed down the row to me. I accepted it and tried not to bring attention to myself.

The Spinners didn't get the Grammy. It went to the Manhattan Transfer, who hadn't had a hit in twenty-five years. I then knew that it was all contrived. The Spinners had a double-sided number one with a bullet hit record "I'll Be Around" and "How Could I Let You Get Away." Well, I guess it is needless to say, I never had a chance to wear my beautiful fifteen-hundred-dollar gown, and Billy had the nerve to be upset with me! I decided that we wouldn't discuss the matter. This was neither the time nor place, but I learned the best lesson that day, which was to listen to my first mind. No matter what he wanted, things had to be done in a timely fashion. His position in life at this point demanded that. The Spinners were nominated several more times, but never won a Grammy Award. Any group that had twelve gold records and a star on the Walk of Fame deserves whatever awards they are nominated for, I felt. I was so happy when they were nominated for the Rhythm and Blues Award. Harvey Fuqua of The Moonglows, their former manager and lifetime friend, was instrumental in that deed. I liked the Rhythm and Blues category because part of the award was monetary, and a crisis fund was also available for those that qualified. Harvey mentioned to me before he passed that he wanted The Spinners to make it into the Rock and Roll Hall of Fame.

Billy and the boys recorded a smash hit record with Dionne Warwick, "Then Came You," and the flip side "Just as Long as We Have Love." This record went gold and got them to Las Vegas on a show with Dionne, playing the Riviera Hotel with their name in lights. They performed for three weeks. I went with them. We stayed in nice bungalows close to the hotel. We invited Dionne and her sister, Dee Dee, over for dinner. I have always liked Dionne.

I asked Dionne what her favorite meal was. She told me chicken and dumplings. I didn't know the first thing about cooking chicken and dumplings. I called my mama and asked her how. Mom was always so willing to see her children succeed she gave me her recipe and the secret to keeping the dumplings light. Everything was a hit with Dionne! She said that the dumplings were the lightest she ever had. She even took some back with her to the hotel.

While we were there, a show was cancelled. Dionne came down with desert throat. Something about the dry sandy desert air affected her throat. After some rest, she was fine.

Las Vegas is family-oriented now. I got to see Fats Domino, famous for singing "Blueberry Hill." I was anxious to meet him. He was one my favorite performers when I was a child. Fats was a very congenial man. It was my honor to make his acquaintance.

Billy got caught up in the gambling. I didn't think it was smart to gamble away the money you were working hard for and go home broke. I mentioned that fact to Billy, and before I knew it, he stopped gambling. I never liked gambling. The money Billy gave to me to gamble with, I bought something at the gift shop, something to take home.

Not long after the Las Vegas gig, Dionne came to Detroit for a gig. She visited the house and had prettiest little girl with her. I asked the child, who was about nine or ten years old, what her name was. She said very politely, "Whitney Houston." I immediately knew from the smile, complexion, and pert little nose that she was Cissy's daughter, Dionne's cousin.

In later years, after Whitney was a megastar, Billy crossed paths with her again. She remembered having been in our home. She told him about what a happy occasion it was for her. Little did we know that the sweet, young lady we entertained in our home would become such a renowned artist.

Everything ran rather smoothly by then. Maybe it was something from Las Vegas, but whatever the case, Billy was came home regularly. We danced together if we heard a song that we liked, no matter what time of day or night, or where we were. It brought me back to that night of roller skating with him in so many ways. When we danced, it felt like we were on a stage meant for just him and I.

One thing that was always in the back of my mind was Billy saying that I would never be bored in our marriage. This sometimes worried me because I don't know in what way he meant it, and I don't think he knew, but it was somewhat exciting and challenging facing the unknown.

I was asked by many a person why was I with Billy. All I know was that from that night at the Duke skating rink that it was meant to be. When you both have feelings at such an early age, those feelings hopefully become renewed in the later years. We even liked same music. Our favorite Spinner song was named "The Winter of Our Love." That was, or should have been gold, a record that was missed by the disc jockeys in *The Labor of Love* album.

My father thought that I deserved a better man. My mother was charmed by Billy. He bought her things. He bought a mink cape for me and suggested that I give it to my mother. He then bought me another mink coat. He knew how to win me over even when we kept having little disagreements here and there. We disagreed anywhere. I remember Buddy Allen saying, "You guys should have a television called *At Home with the Hendersons*. You argue, then you kiss before leaving one another."

And then came another twist from the unknown; the good times seemed harder to come by. I tried to figure it out. Why was this happening again? One thing was, Billy spent lots of money. I thought because I had been a bookkeeper that he would be happy for me to help handle the money he made. Instead he hired my sister Joyce! This seemed strange since he told me that was why he had asked me to quit my job. I felt it was because he made more than he ever imagined. He spent most of it on me. I was given a black mink coat with hat, muff, and a belt purse (it slipped on the belt to the coat). I also got a white fox coat.

Although he bought almost all of my clothing, shoes, and perfumes, he said when I dressed up, he would be embarrassed because I would be so sharp. I thought this was the way a star's wife was supposed to represent him.

There were times when my penchant to come sharp was right on the money though. I finally got a chance to wear my fabulous gown (the $1,500 one) after Billy told me to cut the lining out so it would be a see-through gown. I made a head wrap out of the lining that matched the dress perfectly after I decorated it to match. I wore the dress for two special occasions. One was to a party in Los Angeles given by Atlantic Records Recording Company at the Beverly Hills Hotel. There I met Dana Andrews, who was a very famous star. My father told me that his cousins (husband and wife), were working for Dana as his driver and cook. I never knew this until I began to go to Los Angeles with Billy. When I was introduced to him, I asked him, and he confirmed that they were indeed employed by him. He called their names, Bo and Gert. I was impressed!

The second big occasion was at an African affair called Bel African that was being held at the Henry Ford Mansion. I was invited by Norma (Henry's, of The Spinners, wife). It was a very gala affair that took place on a Saturday afternoon. I arrived with Claudreen (Pervis's wife), and suddenly there was this photographer following me around. He asked me if he could photograph me for the *Free Press* newspaper, which had one of the largest circulations in the state of Michigan. I remember that his name was Dave Turnley. I was flattered and excited to be at the Ford Mansion. Now this handsome, young man was at my every turn while I took a tour of the house. He tried to feed me chocolate-covered strawberries and serve me champagne while asking still if he could photograph me for the newspaper. I accepted and struck a pose while I was outside looking at the boathouse, and the Ford yacht sitting on Lake St. Clair. The front of the mansion faced the lake and was indeed a spectacular view.

The very next day, there I was on the front page of the *Free Press*! What shocked me was, there was a smaller picture of Sophia Loren on the same page. This was my moment! Sophia was one of my very favorite movie stars! My uncle Donny used to call me Sophia Loren! This was truly a thrill for me.

That thrill was cut short when tragedy stuck. Billy's ex-wife passed away, Sterling and Joe's mother. All The Spinners were in town except him. Sterling came to me crying, looking for his father. I stepped in and comforted him. With no way to get in touch with Billy (no cell phones), I had to wait until he showed up. The word spread that Billy's wife passed. My phone blew up with calls from people inquiring if it was me. It was a lot to deal with.

When Billy called, I asked him about the rumor. He said that he didn't know. As he continued to talk, I sensed a coldness that caught me off guard. Somehow he got to talking about his ex-mother in-law in a self-congratulatory tone, as if pleased that the woman would have to deal with him when it came to the arrangements. I later found out that he had something to prove to her mother. He said to her that he would one day be famous, is what he told me. I was embarrassed because he didn't handle the situation with more finesse. I guess he did the best that he knew how.

I had another life lesson: men think differently than women! You can't expect them to ever think like you, like the book titled *Women Are from Venus. Men Are from Mars*. I found out that entertainers fly by their egos most of the time. Life made us all mature faster in different ways, at least I was learning by leaps and bounds.

Chucky and Sterling got married and began having the most beautiful children. Joe, more practical and methodical, was still single. We got the grandchildren (the ones that we knew about) on the weekends when Billy wasn't gigging.

Billy couldn't afford to go to the circus or the State Fairgrounds when he was younger, so it gave him the biggest thrill to be able to take our grandchildren and let them eat and ride the rides as long as they wanted to. They usually did both until they got sick—too much lemonade, cotton candy, corn dogs, etc.

Despite all of the pleasantries, the situation between us got progressively worse. I sensed there were other women, and who knows what else. I didn't want to open that can of worms! I also noticed that if I didn't ask, there was never an explanation for his actions. If I asked, he would tell the truth no matter what. The truth wasn't always easy to take, so I stopped asking. He, in turn, never asked me anything about my whereabouts or anything that might bring him unpleasant information.

One time he didn't come home with the other Spinners, and when he did, I was getting dressed to go out. I got sugar-sharp! I wore my most expensive perfume, put on one of my mink coats, and left as he came in. Little did he know that I had no place to go, so I went to a drive-in movie. I went to the snack bar and filled up on junk food because I forgot to eat during my frustration! I don't remember what the movies were about (back then, you saw two movies and a cartoon for the price of one). It was quite late when I returned home, and the house was lit up like a Christmas tree. I smelled something wonderful that Billy cooked. I wasn't hungry! He looked at me and never said a word except, "Did you have a good time?" I thought, *Mission accomplished*, and answered smugly, "Yes!"

I could never get used to Billy's snoring, so I slept in another bed in another room. The Four Tops knew what I was talking about.

They recorded him asleep and snoring on a road trip. The stewardess would shake Billy and offer him food whenever we flew anywhere. He kept everyone around him awake.

I finally bought another house. It was on same street about seven doors down. We used it for a place to put my clothes and for me to get some peace and quiet. Billy rehearsed the band and new music more frequently at the main house. The idea of my staying over and the houses of neighbors asking to come over and watch rehearsals sounded more and more appealing. What's more, I never knew when he would call these rehearsals. So he got the new home for me. These moves on Billy's part let me know just how much he valued what he needed to do for his career.

By this time, my father, after twenty-six years, was now divorced from mother. He and my stepmother moved to Austin, Texas. After a few more issues with Billy, I went to visit them for a week. The visit out to Austin, Texas, was refreshing, a slower change of pace and scenery. I got along famously with my stepmother, and it was always a treat to see my father. When I returned to Detroit, I discovered that while I was away, Billy let his cousins stay in my house. They took pictures of various persons I had met, a couple of leather outfits, and some turquoise jewelry sets. I asked Billy about the theft, and he promised to get my things back or replace them. He did neither.

I decided I needed to find something to do instead of focusing most of my time and attention on Billy. I applied for an internship with *ABC News*. I did so well I was hired to develop stories for a problem-solving, half-hour segment, which ran for a thirteen-week period!

My career in the field picked up even more from there. After the thirteen weeks were over, I replaced the person (who was out sick) who picked the news headlines off the Reuter ticker tape for that day. I had to be there so very early I placed limitations on myself as far as Billy was concerned. I had to rethink the whole Idea. I loved writing, but it would all have to wait. Billy needed to come first. I bid ABC farewell so I could be available when he wanted me.

And talk about being ahead of one's time. The idea came to me for a sort of television show that would show my life as a star's wife, as I lived it. The show would be called *Barbara's World*. I worked the whole show out with Denise, the writer from England. We sold the idea to Channel 62 in Detroit. The realization of how much of a strain it would put on my time started to dawn on me. The stint with the play, I realized, appealed to me because it was for a limited time only. *Barbara's World* would have been what they call a reality-type show way back then in the eighties and would demand more and more of my time. Billy made the remark, "If you didn't quit work, I wouldn't have you." He was right. I was used to my flexibility and independence, so I stepped away from the project.

I had misgivings in doing so. My mother's favorite saying was, "God bless the child that has its own." This stayed on my mind constantly. During our marriage, I guess there was always a secret need to have my own. I kept the desire to make my own money no matter how generous Billy was. So much of my energy went into making a home life and relations with others comfortable for him.

The Spinners were asked to perform in Acapulco, Mexico. They decided to take their wives. We had a wonderful time. Acapulco was the first place in Mexico that I ever visited. We stayed at The Princess Hotel, in rooms with awe-inspiring views. We were like one large, happy family, entourage included! Then came the cruises!

The Royal Caribbean Cruise worked The Spinners for five years. There was a suite available. The Spinners switched each year so that each one would have a turn. Everything was free to The Spinners and their guests. We got a chance to see Puerto Rico and spend some time there. Billy rented a car, and we rode up to the rain forest. We stopped at a roadside wagon for something to eat. I usually didn't trust eating from those type of places. This day I was so hungry I threw caution to the wind, and was I glad I did. I would have missed some of the tastiest chicken you could have. We went there several times every time we came to Puerto Rico. We drove up to the rain forest to a restaurant with a bar and the most magnificent view. Puerto Rico was one of the main places for the cruise ship to have a day in port. I wasn't the best person when it came to taking pictures, so I decided to buy a charm from wherever I could along my travels. I was such a jewelry nut I bought myself a charm bracelet. Guess what? I don't have a Puerto Rico charm. Who knows? I might make it there again.

St. Thomas was the best place to buy jewelry and perfume, Puerto Rico for liquor. Antigua was where the Disc Jockey Convention was held one year and I had a chance to meet and sit next to Andrew Young, a friend of Martin Luther King Jr., and one-time Mayor of Atlanta, Georgia. Mr. Young was just as gracious as he could be, with his flirtatious self. I was amused. It was all in good, clean fun! Speaking of fun, Antigua was the place for Scotch Bonnet hot sauce, of which Billy and I both liked very much. I learned from Billy that if you can't find it in your hometown, then send for it! I was having the time of my life!

We finally made a trip on the ship to Cozumel, Mexico. I heard this was a romantic place. When the ship docked, three of us wives decided to take a walk and see what was happening in town since it was so close to where we docked. While we strolled, a man approached us and asked if he could be our guide at no cost to us. We quickly discussed it between ourselves and decided that since it was daytime, and we would stay together, the venture was on! I asked the man what his name was and if he knew where a jewelry store was. He said that his cousin owned a jewelry store. We followed him to the store, and I found a piece of smoky topaz, which was sixty karats that I just had to have. I talked the man down to 60 dollars from 150 dollars. I also talked him out of a silver chain. Pervis's wife bought something and got a great deal. He said it was because of his cousin (I don't remember his name). We spent the day there having lunch at another cousin's restaurant; Bobby's wife bought liquor. It was cheaper there. I don't know if the owner was a relative or not, but he knew him quite well!

When we returned to the ship, we found out that they sold the same gemstone for ten dollars a karat. I felt a little guilty. I told our tour guide that I was going to return to have dinner with him. When I left him, he told me that I was so beautiful he wanted to get to know me better. I was flattered, but I couldn't possibly keep the proposed date.

Billy introduced me to the best caviar (the Shah's Golden) and champagne (Dom Perignon) while we were on the cruise. It was far from the cheap, salty kind that you buy in the grocery store. I got hooked fast. We joined the Caviarteria in New York so we could send for it when we wanted some for our anniversary and such. John Edwards, The Spinners' lead singer, bought us a very expensive caviar set. We almost wore it out. It was a gift that was appreciated and well used.

The Spinners now branched out into merchandising. They soon had their own wine label! They had musical get-well cards! Soon there were T-shirts, caps, and Spinner jackets with their names on them. I never got one with my name on it. I never knew why.

The Spinners sang songs in a few movies. They sang in *The Fish That Saved Pittsburgh*, *(Do It, Do It) One Does It Better* starring Dr. J (Julius Irving), Debbie Allen, and Stockard Channing, to name a few. My favorite was the song "Brother to Brother" in the movie *Twins*, starring Danny DeVito and Arnold Schwarzenegger. I could not understand why they didn't include these songs in their show lineup.

They were very excited to find out that they were invited to be guests on *The Bill Cosby Show*. Billy asked me if I wanted to go. Of course, I accepted! Bill Cosby was one of my favorite comedians. When the day came to do the taping, I don't know who was more excited, The Spinners or I. I remember the producers of the show wanted to showcase a particular record, and someone suggested showing a gold record due to their numerous gold records. I walked over to Mr. Cosby during the lull (he was all alone). I wanted to tell him how much I admired his accomplishments.

Before I could open my mouth, he snapped at me, "I am married!"

I replied, "So am I. In fact, that is my husband," pointing at Billy. So much for my input.

That was quite a shock for me, and that's when I became a little reticent about approaching famous people. I realized that a famous person's ego can be incredible. Just because they're famous, doesn't mean they're decent people, as I learned even more so from his dealings with Mr. I'm Married later on (I could've been too conscious at the time for his liking). I met people such as Bob Hope, Leslie Nielsen, Jet Lee, Errol Garner, Barbara Mandrel, Loretta Lynn, Bonnie Raitt, Marvin Gaye, and countless others, and they were far more sociable and kinder when approached by their fans.

The next person I was to meet of world renown fame was jazz pianist, Errol Garner, when I got on the plane from Detroit to New York to be with Billy. I simply adored his work! He never took a piano lesson! As I took my seat, I looked to see who I was next to and quickly looked again. It was Errol Garner, who was known for his composition "Misty," and sitting on a phone book to put him at the proper height to play. Errol laughed and said, "That was the best double take I have ever seen."

While in New York, Billy invited me to New York for dinner with him at Mr. Chow's restaurant for our anniversary. O. J. Simpson was leaving Mr. Chow's as we were entering. Billy introduced me to him. O. J. smiled and kept it moving. He was in a hurry, and it reminded me of the commercial O. J. did, running through the airport to catch a flight. These days, it seems, he was busy running from himself in many ways. Time is an amazing thing.

After dinner, we checked in to the Waldorf Astoria Hotel. Iconic jazz singer, Tony Bennett, was performing. We went to his show, and he was awesome and helped the lack of atmosphere in The Waldorf. The venue was an older, well-established hotel that became famous for its guests.

I got a chance to meet another memorable Errol.

The Spinners were booked in Kingston, Jamaica. Billy suggested I go there a day before. I agreed. When it became time to board Air Jamaica, I was in the airport bar. I heard the flight being announced, so I proceeded to the gate and was barely seated on the plane when I heard my name being announced over the loud speaker saying I won the right to fly with the crew in the cockpit. The stewardess escorted me to the cockpit. I said I didn't know how I had been chosen, but I was very happy because I had secretly always wanted to fly with the crew.

They told me that I was the second person to board, so I had been chosen. I knew this wasn't true because I was the last to board. Whatever the reason, I was thrilled. I met the pilot, who was named Errol, and the navigator. Another Errol, what were the chances? I sat back, relaxed, and enjoyed the opportunity.

When we landed, I tried to get transportation to the hotel we were supposed to stay. Errol saw me and asked me if I would feel safe riding with him. I felt safe enough to fly with him, so a ride to the hotel seemed reasonable. On the way to the hotel, I kept seeing these signs advertising jerk chicken and jerk pork. I asked what the signs meant. Errol laughed so hard.

He said, "You don't know jerk?"

I said, "No."

He told me that he would show me rather than try to explain. He dropped me off at the hotel and later called to see if The Spinners had arrived. I informed him that the guys were due in the next day. He asked me if I would like a tour of Kingston, not on the tourists' path. I said yes. In the meantime, I found out that jerk was a special seasoning that was spicy and used to season grilled chicken and pork cooked over pistachio wood. The taste made me hum with delight.

Errol said he would pick me up around seven o'clock because I shouldn't spend my first night in Kingston alone. He also let me know he was unattached at the moment. I reminded him that my husband was arriving the next day, and that was the only reason I was in Jamaica. I let the clerk at the front desk of the hotel know I was leaving and with whom. Of course, Errol was well known in Jamaica, being a pilot.

There was a multi-Rastafarian party on the beach that night. We went! We ate jerk food, danced, and smoked marijuana out of cow horns. The party lasted till the early morning! When I got back the hotel, there was just enough time to change and greet Billy and the entourage! There were people waiting to take my picture for a travel magazine. I took pictures but never saw the outcome.

The guys arrived and had the same questions about jerk. By this time, I was an expert on both the jerk and weed (hey, this was

Jamaica after all). I did so well they wanted to send me ahead as an ambassador for them.

The mountains of Jamaica were fascinating and beautiful. I saw my first double rainbow after a midday tropical shower. It was a wondrous time to see people of color functioning in such a picturesque setting. It was like living on a perpetual vacation.

Not long after Jamaica, Dick Clark set up a bus tour for The Spinners throughout the south. Dick was producing an album on them. Billy asked me along. I went, not realizing that I had to ride the bus with all these men. Pervis gave me his bed on the bus so I could be close to Billy. He crowded in with the band members. It turned out to be quite nice. Everybody was happy to have a female along. They all catered to me. Everything was fine until I woke up the next day and panicked. I looked around me, and there was wood all around. I said to myself, "They have buried me, and I'm not even dead!" I went to sleep tired from vodka and the silliest sing-alongs with some of the guys. That vodka must have been serious because I didn't remember anything of how the bunk looked after I got in it. I just wanted some sleep!

On this tour, Billy had an appreciation for my interest in history and remembered I did the play *Selma*. When we got to Memphis, he took me to the Lorraine Hotel and showed me the room that Martin Luther King Jr. had been assassinated in front of (which was all that was available to African Americans back then). I remember a sweltering heaviness coming over me, coupled with a sickening sense of rage. This still affects me today. I marched with him in Detroit.

It appeared that Billy began to arrange things for me to take part in to keep me, shall we say, distracted. Trips came and went where I wasn't invited. I asked questions and got few answers. I found solace in few things. While I watched helplessly, our marriage slowly began to fall apart. I became somewhat lonesome and craved companionship.

I felt left out and neglected. Stroking the fur of a mink or sipping Dom Perignon did little to ease the pain. I totally understand those bored, well-kept white women married to successful men who were out enjoying themselves. Billy was doing his thing more and more. I could feel it so sharply my spine would go cold in the middle of the night. Determined to fight fire with fire, I had a few indiscretions, but they did nothing for me. I filed for divorce. This was happening at the same time The Spinners had a new release. It was titled, ironically, "You Go Your Way, I'll Go Mine."

Billy was so wrapped in what he was doing he didn't know I had filed. Someone showed him a copy of *The Hollywood Reporter*, where I filed. It was in *The Michigan Chronicle*, the African American newspaper in Detroit.

The announcement got his attention! It got not only his, but the attention of the group, the record company, and others was focused on us. All income stopped. Atlantic records called Buddy Allen. In turn, Buddy called Billy and asked him what was going on. My attorney put a hold on all transactions in lieu of the upcoming divorce.

Billy was furious! He threatened me and ranted and raved. The Spinners were on his back about not getting any money. They told him he had to do something! Finally, we had a serious talk. I wasn't really ready for a divorce, and neither was he. So we confessed that we both loved each other but couldn't get along because we were both strong-willed and controlling. Billy asked me if I heard the phrase, "I am in love with a bitch I can't stand." I told him I never of heard that before, and I was not a female dog—a bitch! Yet I knew exactly what he meant because I felt the same way. After all, who was really putting where it was with dog-like behavior? We laughed a hard, weary laugh. It broke the ice of long-grinding tension between us.

Billy was not used to a wife, and I wasn't used to a husband. Maybe that was why I had four before him. Being married to him was exciting adventurous, romantic, all of which I liked, but I never knew it was so much work!

My favorite escape from bad situations was simply to escape! I didn't like arguing about anything, although it always seemed that I was the one to disagree with him. I would forget at times that though we both came from the projects; our backgrounds were entirely different. Billy loved me but didn't respect me like I needed to be respected. Eventually, we worked things out, and I stopped the divorce proceedings. Things were strained between us, but we soon got better.

Billy invited me out with him more often. He said that I was his "brown sugar." I remember small things like him calling, "Hey, Barb," or him warming up for a show and dancing to Earth, Wind & Fire's song "Boogie Wonderland." It always fascinated me how light he was on his feet. He was chubby but outdanced the other Spinners.

Right around the same time that this mess with Billy and me was happening, Jackie Wilson was in the hospital. The Spinners decided to have a benefit for him at the Latin Casino in Cherry Hill, New Jersey. I decided to keep up appearances in the style I was known for with a beige satin nightgown. It had a cocoon, short-sleeved satin jacket with marabou feather trim. The gown was long with a split on the side. I had crocheted a skullcap that was gold-and-silver thread filled with jewels crocheted all over. Just so you know, I wore jeweled hats before Cher. The way I saw it, my outfit and presentation could remind Billy of how good he had it with me by his side. Cecil Franklin once told me, "Barbara, you bring Hollywood to Detroit." I smiled and thanked him. I hoped it was a compliment.

We continued to work on the marriage, although I halfway thought that he reconciled with me because of the money situation. At the same time, I still felt the love from him, and I knew I loved him.

While we went through our ups and down, so was my weight. It was a constant battle. I followed Billy in trying different foods. The strain of what was happening in my life created a need for the comfort of food.

I watched Sterling and Caroline (CeeCee, our middle son, and his wife). Their marriage wasn't perfect, yet I could see a common bond between them. I don't know why, but I went to the kids and asked them what it was that they knew that I didn't. They asked me if I would go to Bible class with them. I said to myself, "Why not? It certainly can't hurt. Yes." I believe it was on a Tuesday night the next week. I went over to the house early because I suddenly felt an urgency to make sure that I didn't miss this event.

When we arrived at this institute, people were quick to give an embrace and offer kind words. After we were seated, I noticed a chalkboard with the words, Yahweh, Elohim, Yahshua, and under these words, Father, Word or Son, Holy Ghost. Then there were these words, Lord, God, Jesus Christ, and under these words was, Erroneous. Seeing this frightened me because this is all I knew all my life. I thought maybe this was a cult. I remember hearing about Jim Jones and the 1978 mass suicides he set up with his followers in Guyana. *How could I get these kids out of here?* I thought.

As if reading my mind, the person speaking said, "With a little research, you will find this information to be true."

They drew a symbol on the board, and I copied it. When I went home that night, I could only find my American Heritage Dictionary, not my Bible. I looked up the Tetragrammaton, the four Hebrew letters used as a symbol for God's name Yahweh. I knew that this was the truth, and I would never be the same. I didn't how if I would tell Billy about this Bible class at the institute. Somehow I knew when the time came that I would be led the right thing to do.

Well, the time came soon enough! One night we were having a decent conversation. I don't quite remember what it was about. Somehow religion became the topic. I decided to tell Billy about the Bible classes I had been attending with the kids. He told me he had been Lutheran. Amazing how some things can float in a relationship and never be discussed.

I asked him what was God's name. He paused for a moment and said, "God."

I then asked what the son's name was. He thought again and then said, "Jesus."

He looked a bit puzzled while I asked what was the name of the Holy Ghost. He answered, quite angrily and unsure, "Jesus."

All these questions were answered in the Bible classes I attended, relative to the names of the Father, (Word) or Son, and the Holy Ghost. I wondered what true god I was serving because there are so many. When I found out that Yahweh was the name of the one and only true god, I breathed that name; the revelation of this knowledge rang true in my inner being, (Elohim)! It all made sense to me. I was excited, a little frightened, yet ready to tell him and everyone else what I was learning.

Billy decided to check out the Bible classes. He later told me he just knew I was seeing an older man. Hah! If he only knew. He continued to attend with me every time he was in town. We both noticed how integrated the classes were. We also noticed there was never a collection plate passed around at any time. Very intriguing.

I began to notice a difference in the both of us. We began to calm down when talking to each other. We became less guarded. We both respected the truth. The Spinners and everyone concerned noticed the difference. They wanted to know what happened to calm us both at the same time.

Billy wanted to know the whereabouts of the other like-minded institutes. He wanted to continue to attend wherever he was gigging. He found out there were classes or schools all over the United States and overseas. He purchased a set of pictorial charts to take with him with his Bible on the road. He began telling his friends and all who would listen about his newfound knowledge. As in all the schools, the charts were a teaching aid. He began to record the lectures so that he could remember them and use them also as a teaching aid.

Our lives became more sedate! I lost some weight! Things were good, proof that our focus was on more important things.

One Sunday there was a guest speaker named Dr. Glenn W. Kinley, who spoke at the institute where I attended. I found out that he was a son of the man who started the Bible classes, Dr. Henry C. Kinley. He lectured in such a way that was humorous yet included many truths. I told Billy about him and how Glenn's father had a vision and revelation.

Not long after I had met Dr. Kinley, Billy flew me to Los Angeles on my fiftieth birthday. We went to Mr. Chow's Restaurant to dinner. Later we went to visit the class in Los Angeles and had a desire to visit the class in Pasadena. Billy and I asked his sister, Edna, who lived in Los Angeles, how far Pasadena was from where she lived and if she would take us there to attend a class. She was more than willing to drive there. She enjoyed the lecture. We were asked if we had any questions at its end. She said that she didn't have any, but her brother did. Billy was so embarrassed because he was overwhelmed with knowledge that he suddenly forgot what it was he wanted to know. We laughed because he was so excited and told us he had questions to be answered.

The next thing I knew, Billy was asking me if I wanted to move to California. Well, to be more specific, he asked me one night when I was going to move. The next day I called Dr. Kinley in California and told him our desire to move to where he was so that we could attend his classes.

I always wanted to live in California. I was told it was so expensive to live there. I had a conversation with Billy explaining that he would have to pay the rent and expenses wherever I stayed, in addition to keeping up the expenses in Detroit since I was unemployed. He agreed as long as I attended the Bible classes and learned everything I could. This was fine with me since I had insatiable thirst for knowledge.

As we got involved with the classes, there were some very disturbing news concerning the true name of Yahweh. In Florida there was cult using the name incorrectly. They were making a profit in some of the worst ways in the name of a so-called prophet called Yahweh Ben Yahweh, which translated, means Yahweh, Son of Yahweh. They fleeced people out of their money, cutting ears off, and people were getting killed, according to what I read in the newspapers.

This was so far from what I was taught and researched. One of the first things that I ever heard before was the meaning of the Tetragrammaton (or the four Hebrew letters transliterated and used as a symbol for the name of God, YHWH). Since consonants are unpronounceable without vowels, an A and E were inserted to not only make it pronounceable, but show Adam and Eve being both masculine and feminine within one embodiment, as we all are. This was the beginning of my understanding of how we were made in the likeness and image of our creator.

This excited me and inspired my thirst for more knowledge! Billy and I fully agreed on something without controversy! This also excited me. We both looked forward to a new beginning in California and learning what we could from the teachings of the Institute.

In the meantime, Billy got a chance to meet Dr. Glenn Kinley and his wife on one of their visits to the Detroit class. We invited them to stay with us whenever they happened to be in Detroit. The invitation was accepted. Billy and I felt quite privileged and, most of all, blessed. With them there, I felt that I could learn how to be as well.

We got in a few private sessions at our home, whereby we could invite others, such as the drummer for The Spinners band, Theodore Smith, and anyone else who wanted to attend. We made a couple of trips more to California and attended classes.

I finally moved to California. I moved with a single woman by the name of Celeste. She was very friendly and receptive, and I loved her as a soul mate immediately. We found out that we had a lot in common, including a mutual friend, Barbara Harris of Atlantic Records.

Billy never moved to California. He commuted there from wherever and whenever he had a chance. I wound up living there for about six or seven years. We both received licenses to teach and lecture about what we were taught and, most of all, believed.

My mother came out there after I got a place of my own. She stayed a month at a time. These were some of the best times that I can remember in my life. We took walks together. She attended classes with me when she felt like it. She began to understand what I was learning. Things were going great.

Billy's sister, Edna, gave us an old, maroon Chevy she had for us to use. She just purchased a Lincoln Town Car and saw no point letting the other sit idle. We didn't have to buy a car since we had one in one in Detroit. Thank you, (Cookie) Edna! I love you for being so thoughtful. I remember Billy was getting ready to visit me and called to ask me about some weed or marijuana. I told him I didn't know where to get any. The only people that I knew were in the Bible class, and I certainly wasn't going to ask around. He said that he would make a few calls and call me back. He did. He told me that the road manager for The Temptations would be calling me.

Somebody, whose name I don't even remember, called and said he would meet me somewhere between Pasadena and Los Angeles to bring me a package for Billy. I asked him how would we know each other. He told me that he would be driving a brown Peugeot. I told him that I would be driving an old Chevy with the roof lining hanging down. Hey, a free car, no car payments. I didn't care what it looked like. I believed Billy and never questioned the situation concerning the so-called package. That was one of the most ridiculous moves I ever made. Oh, the things we do for love. Luckily, everything worked out.

California was good for us, or should I say, for me, in that I not only was I learning things I never heard before, it was refreshing to be in fair weather and not deal with Detroit's thick and chilling winters. It was breathtakingly beautiful getting up with the sun every day! I felt inspired to get a job!

I knew Billy would object, but I had to keep my independence and make my own money. I found out that if I worked, I kept my self-esteem and didn't have to ask anyone for money. He would just have to understand. I went to a casting company and got a job as an extra in the made-for-television movie *Please Take My Daughters*, starring Rue Mclanahan of the TV show *Golden Girls*. I met Rue during a lunch. She was one of the most personable people I was ever to meet in my lifetime. She encouraged me to pursue my dream. I returned to the casting company after the completion of the movie. Upon realizing that I couldn't keep driving there with the hope that I would be chosen to be an extra that day and repeat the procedure every day; I had to do something that offered more stability.

I heard that Security Pacific Bank in Glendale, California, which wasn't far from Pasadena, was hiring customer service representatives. Since I hadn't worked for a while, I thought this would be a good place to start. I applied and was accepted for a position in that department. It was wonderful! I not only had a chance to hone my people skills, I talked to DeForest Kelly's (Bones of *Star Trek*) wife. She was such a delightful person to talk with. I was at work again and was making a salary at something I enjoyed.

I soon made manager and then supervisor. I attended Bible classes at least three times a week and still traveled with Billy. My schedule felt satisfying and fully realized. I began to notice some things happening. Billy was being booked quite a few gigs within drivable distance in California.

They were so hot, record-wise, I saw Billboards with them showing their latest number-one record. Having grown up with them, I was excited for them, both as a wife and a childhood friend. Then came the star on the Hollywood Walk of Fame. I got to see places like Laguna Niguel, which was very pictorial. Just driving from place to place to be with Billy was exhilarating, educational, and very scenic.

I was in the Bible class approximately nine or ten years when I noticed there were no illnesses or deaths in the class. Remember, I ran in the entertainment circles where excess, drugs, and the like ran people into the ground, so the lack of death and sickness here was not only amazing, but strange. This was a class size of over about two hundred people!

While taking notice of such things, I saw an ad promoting the opportunity to become a real estate agent. Being a realtor always interested me (I played with doll houses with that emphasis in mind as a child). I went to real-estate school after work and eventually became an agent for Hawkins Realty in Pasadena. They say that to get a license to sell real estate in California was really tough. I took the test and was told that I passed with flying colors. You are never told your score, just if you passed or failed.

I was not the only one growing in leaps and bounds. The Pasadena Institute of Divine Metaphysical Research, Inc. was moving to a larger place, and Dr. Kinley and his family decided to move, so I was given their home for my first sell! I can't explain how grateful I was for the opportunity. I learned so much because I was given the chance to exercise what I learned in more ways than one.

When Billy came for a visit, I gave him a thousand dollars from my commission. I thought he would be proud of me because of my accomplishments. I was wrong. He wasn't happy at all. I then remembered his saying, "If I didn't have you quit work, I wouldn't have you." He didn't realize that it was *what I needed*. He felt threatened with my so-called freedom.

After I became gainfully employed, things seemed to change in a way I can't explain. Somehow Billy thought he had something to prove not only to me, but to everyone. In his mind, it was hard for him to believe that someone like me could ever love and depend on him. After all this time! I know because he told me so.

Now our relationship became strained even though we had the Bible class in common. He continued to take me with him. The whole class went on vacations together. I remember one trip was to Big Bear Mountain in California. I heard about this place and was more than excited to go. Billy had to work. He did something I couldn't understand and didn't like. He gave his brother, Louis, a credit card to take care of my expenses while I was there. I resented this move on his part. I was glad that I was working and had my own money. He wasn't spoiling my fun and new adventure. If he couldn't be there, he still wanted to control me, so he knew money would be the best way. It didn't work. I did get everything taken care of. My money was free to do as I pleased, and I had a complete ball!

The class went on our next trip to Desert Hot Springs, California. The weather was balmy and quite pleasant. Some of us went to some resale shops, and I found a fur stole that was almost new and inexpensive. The weather wasn't nearly as hot as it could have been. Almost everyone laughed at me for buying furs in the desert. I think they were jealous because I got such a deal. It was quite cool in California in the evenings, so I had a chance to wear all of my furs. Yes, indeed, Billy kept forgetting that he was husband number five, and that I knew how to take care of myself.

Another twist and turn came from the Bible class. After a while, Dr. Kinley decided to move to Florida. He told us that he had sheep in Florida. I was happy about the move because I would be closer to my family. Billy was happy because it was closer to Detroit, where he was still living. Most of the Bible class made the move in order to continue to learn more of the truth.

I moved back to Detroit because Billy and I had not talked about the move to Florida. He never moved to California as I spoke of earlier. He said to me one day, "I am supposed to be the star, but I seem to be following you." His ego made him forget that the California move was our decision. Now the purpose for the move changed for him.

While I was in Detroit, we received a call from Gary and Brenda Groves, who were in the Pasadena class. They established residence in Ormond Beach, Florida, and extended an invitation for us to visit them. I gave it some thought because Billy was still working and couldn't make a decision due to his restrictions.

Then The Spinners were asked to perform at Disney World's grand opening with Regis Philbin and Kathy Lee Gifford. It was to take place for New Years'. I was pretty clueless to the holidays because I was thinking solely about the invite from the Groves and the Florida weather.

Everything went well at the performance, and it was time to head back to Detroit. I called the Groves and asked if the invitation was still open and how long I could stay. It was perfect weather in Florida compared to the freezing cold in Detroit. The Groves said I could stay as long as I wanted. Their home was my home. It reminded me of the Spanish saying, *"Mi casa es su casa."* I then informed Billy that I would be going to Florida for the visit and returning to Detroit in the springtime. He wasn't too happy, but he definitely understood.

I wound up staying for a year. I began looking for a place of my own. I attended Bible classes in wonderful, balmy weather. Billy, in the meantime, had bars on the windows and steel doors installed in the house in Detroit, something his road manager turned him on to. When I went back to Detroit, my decision to buy a home in Florida was confirmed. I refused to live like a prisoner in my own home, looking out of a window with bars.

Of course, Billy didn't take to the idea. He didn't have a choice as far as I was concerned. I started to make preparations to move. While Billy had to work, I began to get rid of everything I could. Finally, one day he said to me, "Well, I guess it's time to move. The refrigerator and stove are gone." I guess when the food situation shifted, he came to the conclusion that I was serious.

I hired someone to drive me and my pregnant dog to Florida. The neighborhood mutt had gotten to her (as I spoke of earlier). I hadn't found a place yet. I settled into Groves' home with their two dogs and my pregnant dog. The Groves were happy and welcomed us with open arms.

We decided on what would be fair as rent, and my new life started. Almost everything except my clothes went into storage. Our furs, Billy's and my various kinds, were stored in an anvil case until we could find someone who stored furs. Living in Florida, we didn't know when we would have a use for them.

Billy liked the setup because all he did was come home, and everything was done. This all worked for a while. Although the Groves were wonderful, I realized that I wasn't used to living with anyone else. After about a year was when I started to look for our own home. I thought that I could get Billy to help.

Bobby and Lorraine, his wife, were looking for a place in the Orlando area and found a really lovely place. Billy wasn't good at looking at homes, so he left it up to me. I didn't want a place as large as what Bobby and Lorraine had. I wanted something small but comfortable. I finally found a house at the end of a dead-end street in a small suburb of Daytona Beach. It was for sale! This was great because Fred (The Spinners' light man) sold realty and agreed to sell our house in Detroit. In no time flat, he called us and told us he had an interested buyer.

I said to myself that if the house in Florida was supposed to be ours, then it would still be there when I returned after closing the deal in Detroit. It was still there. Hallelujah! That was the sign I needed. The move to Florida went well because Billy and I were closer. We went to Bible-class meetings together whenever we could. I still traveled whenever he invited me. One of the big trips for me was a trip to Hawaii. They were performing on the island Maui. It was a truly colorful place to be. Some friends traveled with us. I got to explore some places with them. Billy wasn't interested because it was quite expensive to be there, and he never did much whenever he worked.

Florida was somewhat strange for us. It seemed to me, and maybe I'm wrong, that Billy felt restricted because of the Gospel, or this amazing truth we were learning. Before the Bible classes, he was a wheeler dealer of sorts. This great knowledge didn't allow him to think as he was used to thinking prior to it.

Chucky moved from California with my granddaughter, Aliyah, to Florida. He had been in touch with Philippe's oldest son, Emanuel. Ava, Emanuel's mother and Philippe's ex-wife, and I have always tried to keep in touch with each other. She lost her younger son, Alvarez, the result of a drive-by shooting in California, and I figured a change of scenery could be good for her.

Emanuel sounded exactly like his father, adlib and all, when he sang. He came to Florida to collaborate with Chuck in their singing. Emmanuel started going to the Bible class. He got a job as a telemarketer. Emanuel was such a gentle, loving, giving person. I loved him so much.

One day, Emanuel, who was just twenty-six years old at the time, rode a bus home when he witnessed a car going into a retention pond filled with water. He made a decision to try and help the occupant of the car. He and someone else got off the bus and jumped in the water. He drowned trying to help the driver get out of the car.

When the driver of the car was asked how he felt about someone losing their life trying to save him, he was very indifferent saying, "Things happen." I felt so bad I could barely talk to Ava. I felt helpless because it seemed to happen on my so-called watch. She lost both of her children so tragically. We could not understand how this happened because Emanuel could swim.

People placed a memorial where the tragedy happened. Emanuel was recognized as a hero from the Daytona Beach fire department. He was awarded the prestigious Carnegie Hero Fund Commission medal for bravery. I accepted it in his mother's stead since she hadn't come to Daytona yet.

After about a year, the memorial disappeared, and the retention pond was filled in.

I remembered that I was in the south, and an African American saved a white person. As pretty as Daytona was, racism was still very much alive. When I see memorials along the highways or wherever, I am reminded of such injustices and wonder what the race of the victim was.

One morning Billy prepared to leave for a gig in Las Vegas when he told me he had trouble breathing. I wanted him to cancel the trip and go and see a doctor. Of course, he refused because the gig was too important. He left home with me worrying and promised to call when he got in Vegas. Billy never got to Las Vegas.

The plane had to make an emergency landing in Dallas, Texas. He was taken off the plane and rushed to the hospital. Upon examination, he was found to be in need of a quadruple heart bypass. The doctor attending Billy called me and suggested that I take the next flight to Dallas. He explained that Billy was in terrible shape and in a near-death situation. One valve in his heart was 95 percent clogged. Another valve was 75 percent clogged. I couldn't remember the blockage in another valve. I almost blacked out as I stood with the phone to my ear. That other valve was, I'm sure, also bad.

For some unknown reason, I wasn't packing or making reservations to leave. This frightened me because I knew that I loved my husband, but I wasn't rushing to be by his side. What was happening to me?! I usually knew exactly what to do in an emergency!

I called the head of the Bible class, Dr. Glenn Kinley, to let him know what was happening with Billy. He was already aware. He said for me to tell Billy to come home. Billy called back, and I told him what I was told, that he should come home. He, devoid of his humor and quick responses, agreed, almost breathless. He wanted to talk to Dr. Kinley to confirm my conversation with him. His remarks to me were, "Not that I don't believe you, baby."

Not long after these conversations took place, I received a call from Billy's doctor saying it would be better if I could fly there because it would be too dangerous for Billy to fly. He wouldn't be responsible if Billy chose to leave the hospital. Billy signed himself out of the hospital. Later he told me that Dr. Kinley told him to come home, that he would be with him all the way.

I received a call from a wonderful person by the name of Thelma Jenkins, (if I remember her name correctly; and I pray that I do), a fantastically patient, kind, and sensitive employee of Delta Airlines. She informed me that although Billy never completed his flight due to the detour to the hospital, she would see to it that he flew back to Daytona Beach. Her husband, Philip, would be assisting him.

Billy flew back with Philip at his side. My heart ached when I met Billy at the airport, with stubble about his usually clean-shaven face. A look of wrenching withdrawal clouded his usually dark, mischievous eyes. I smiled, well, I tried to, but a hard, painful swallow cut it short. I realized why I hesitated in going to Dallas. I wasn't prepared to see him struck down like this. He was always my go-to for adventure. My legs got weak. My man. What had life done to my man?

I tried to get Philip to have dinner with us and spend the night. My hope was that he would help me brace myself for everything that would be required of me. He refused and told me Billy kept talking about a Bible class he had to attend. Philip had a turnaround flight leaving within the hour, so as soon as Billy was in my hands, he left.

My nephew, Michael, who was a truck driver at the time, just happened to come in town. He was with me when I went to pick Billy up from the airport. I didn't want any mistakes with checking to see that he was okay, so I told Billy that we were going to the hospital. He said he wanted to stop at home first.

As we rode toward home, Billy kept talking about how good he felt and that he didn't have to go to the hospital. When I found out that Billy refused to go, I appealed to Dr. Kinley to help me get Billy to go. Dr. Kinley explained to us that he had Billy come back home because recovery time would be extensive after the type of surgery he was to have. He then told Billy to go in to the hospital now! I gave Billy the evil eye. Billy was obedient and went.

Dr. Kinley was right. A quadruple bypass was a serious operation. This was Billy's first time being sick and being hospitalized. He was scared beyond words, and I slipped in and out of a dumfounded state of shock.

The Spinners were very supportive and continued Billy's salary uninterrupted. He recovered slowly but fully. I, in turn, was able to laugh here and there again. Ugh! He, this man, worried me so. Nevertheless, I was proud of how he recovered. Billy lost weight and tried to change his eating habits. It was very hard for him to continue his healthy eating because as a child, he was always hungry enough to eat whatever he could find.

He began to eat at Bob Evan's Restaurant. The manager of the Daytona eatery liked Billy and learned to prepare his food just the way he liked it. This was good for me because he was used to eating out. All I had to do was accompany him to the restaurant. The downside of Billy's operation was that he became a diabetic, and his kidneys began to fail. Now eating healthy had to be a way of life.

After Dr. Glenn Kinley's transition, or death in 1997, things began to change. In fact, I had a stroke that left me partially but temporarily paralyzed on my right side. I never saw it coming. I went to bed the night before and woke up about 4 o'clock in the morning feeling strange. Billy happened to be home, so I woke him out of his sleep to tell him so; and he said try to go back to sleep, that maybe I was having a bad dream. I assured him that wasn't it, but I couldn't figure out what it was. I lied down again, but something told me not to go back to sleep. My right arm felt heavy.

One of the friends who had gone to Hawaii with us was a doctor (Dr. Dan Warner). I called him, and he told me to immediately go to the hospital. I woke Billy, who had gone back to sleep again, and told him we had to go to the hospital right away. Suddenly I couldn't dress myself. Billy took one look at my face as it began to twist. He panicked. He had to help me dress. I was so glad I had a loose-fitting muumuu type dress to put on.

As I walked to the car, I was suddenly dragging my right leg. I tried to stay as calm as possible for Billy's sake. Something in my mind kept telling me it was all from stress. He was trying to carry me. I suggested that if he would just help me, I could walk. When we arrived at the hospital, I probably would have gone through the admittance process quicker if I didn't have so much jewelry on. I was given an envelope to put in everything I was wearing. Billy just shook his head, blinking like an exhausted and bewildered child.

It seemed that everyone from the Bible class came to see me all at once. They kept coming, so much so that the hospital staff wanted to know who I was. I was so grateful for the love. It encouraged me to really try to get myself together.

Billy was so frightened when I looked at him, he had tears in his eyes.

He said to me, "I always wanted to die before you."

I told him indignantly, "You still may have that chance. I am not going any place."

We both laughed!

I had to work really hard to get back to being somewhat normal. I couldn't understand what happened that suddenly my life was so different. I was told I would never be the same. I found this out for myself when I went to Memphis, Tennessee, for a New Year's gig. I had the stroke in November, and I thought I was fine, so I went with Billy to the gig that a wonderfully kind person named Bonnie Sugarman booked.

I thought I was doing all right until I got on the elevator that evening. I suddenly felt frightened of the people I didn't know that were in the elevator. I had trouble breathing. My mouth went dry. I couldn't control the tears; I was so frightened. The other Spinner wives were in the elevator with me. They gathered around me. I felt safe and stopped crying. This really puzzled me because I was always a people person. I usually gravitated to people and spoke to just about everyone. Just as I calmed down and got off the elevator, I noticed the duck parade.

I remember they stayed at the Peabody Hotel. There were these ducks that marched on a red carpet to the hotel fountain in the lobby of the hotel for a swim. They stayed in a penthouse and would be escorted in the elevators to the lobby at eleven o'clock in the morning and five o'clock in the evening. The guests sometimes fed them. After their swim, they would be escorted back to the elevators to return back to the penthouse. I calmed myself down by then.

We went to where the venue was, and the wives all told Billy what happened to me in the elevator. He asked them to keep an eye on me while he performed. After the show, he kept me near him and introduced me to several people, including Bonnie Sugarman, the senior vice president of Agency for Performing Arts (APA), one of the largest diversified talent agencies in Los Angeles with headquarters in Beverly Hill, New York, Nashville, Atlanta, and London.

I was all right because I was mostly surrounded by familiar faces.

I know now that it was too soon to be out on the road with Billy. It takes months, sometimes years, to recover. Some people never get back to so-called *normal.* Simply put, I was blessed and highly favored with my recovery.

In my race back to independence, I tried to take care of my household chores. I found myself transposing numbers, going over every check that I wrote, and whatever else there was when dealing with numbers. Telephone numbers, addresses—it was as if numbers became an obsession. I learned that this was one of the results of the stroke. There would be more to follow. I tried smoking cigarettes after the stroke, then I remembered that smoking constricted the blood vessels. I said to myself that I was too blessed to have recovered as well as I had and was still recovering. What a fool I would be to continue putting my health in jeopardy. I quit immediately and never went through withdrawal. I just stopped cold turkey, like my dad, who stopped drinking and smoking the same day. I said to myself, "I have his genes."

On a lighter note, Billy said he knew when I was much better because I started making out checks again. We were coming back to our daily routine.

The Spinners were booked to go to Athens, Greece. It was about six months after I had the stroke. I felt a lot better. I had not gone anywhere with Billy after New Year's. Athens, Greece? I just knew that I was ready. Wrong.

I felt lighter on my feet thinking about going to Greece. Billy invited me, and I said yes before he finished the question. The flight was long but not exhausting. I felt weak and burdensome in that we both were wheeled about in wheelchairs. Imagine that. I couldn't keep up walking because I was still recovering, and my leg was weak. Remember, I said I felt lighter on my feet. Well, make that felt. Billy resorted to wheelchairs after his heart bypass.

When we arrived in Athens, we stayed at a hotel with a view of the Parthenon, the Acropolis, etc. The wives decided that we were definitely going to visit this historical place. My girlfriend, Joyce Heath, from the Bible class was on hand for the trip, paying her own way so as to not impose.

The day that we (the girls) decided to visit the Parthenon was a beautiful day. We proceeded to pay our way to the former temple and found out that you were basically on your own. There were stairs that were very narrow and almost straight up to the Parthenon. I took one look at how we were to get to the top and broke out in a sweat. This, again, was another sign that I was not well from the stroke. Thoughts ran wild in my head. Did I really fly all the way over to Greece to stand (or sit) before these sites and imagine going in with everyone else? Would I ever fully recover?

I felt that I couldn't make it unless there was some sort of some railing to hold onto. So I decided to wait at the bottom until the girls returned. They all asked me if I would be all right. Of course, I replied that I would be fine. I was tired of being the invalid. They started the climb.

While I was sitting there waiting for them to return, it dawned on me that this was a once-in-a-lifetime opportunity. I might not have this chance again. So I decided to take my time and climb the stairs to one of the most historic sites. When I reached the other women, they were quite surprised to see me. As I looked around, my mind went back to some of the things I was taught in school concerning the Parthenon. They coincided with the things I was taught in the Bible class.

Construction was being done to restore the Parthenon, this temple dedicated to the goddess Athena of Greek mythology. There were pieces of chips of marble on the ground. I picked up some pieces for souvenirs for myself and the other ladies. I had my piece of marble made into a pendant. I don't know what they finally did with their chips. Billy, Joyce, and I wanted to go to the Isle of Patmos to visit where the Book of Revelation was written by Apostle John. The hotel concierge was against the trip. It would be longer there and back than we had the time before our departure back to America.

We opted for the Isle of Mykonos, which was closer to Athens by a hydrofoil boat. I had never been on a hydrofoil. I saw them in the movies. A hydrofoil has vanes or foils attached to the hull to lift the boat out of the water to gain speed.

Mykonos was a beautiful place for tourists. Billy didn't go on the trip. Joyce and I had lunch and started looking for souvenirs to take back. The souvenirs that we priced were overpriced, almost three times what we would pay in Athens. We found the pier for the return trip, and we made ourselves comfortable. I felt so historic, so biblical, in fact, being among the ancient architecture, but not enough to accept their prices. We agreed that if we knew more about Mykonos, we would not have gone to it.

Greece was my last trip out of the country. Things with The Spinners seemed to start to become strained after Greece. Billy, for starters, returned to his old eating habits. Soon the diabetes got worse, and he had to go on insulin, needle and all. He wanted me to give him his injections. I couldn't because I wasn't on the road with him. He had to learn to do it himself. He was so angry that he had to do the injections himself. I had seen him angry, but never like this, all red-faced and bloated. I explained to him that it was his illness, and he had to do it himself. My advice went over like a lead balloon! He didn't take care of himself like he did when he had the heart bypass. It seemed to be too much work for him.

Before you knew what was happening, Billy was told that he was having a serious kidney failure problem, and he would have to go on dialysis. I took the news like a hammer to the face and reminded myself of what stress could do to my condition, which would make me useless to help Billy. The doctor suggested peritoneal dialysis so that he could have a certain quality of life. Peritoneal dialysis is done through the inside lining called the peritoneum of the abdominal cavity. Your belly acts as a natural filter. Wastes are taken out by means of a cleansing fluid called dialysate, which is done through a tube placed in the stomach. This can be done at home or where it is convenient. It is portable. There was a special machine that warmed the fluid and did the exchange. Billy had a case with wheels made so that he could take the machine with him.

Billy and I took classes to further understand the procedure. He wound up traveling with the machine that provided his ability to have dialysis and be able to perform on stage. He took the initiative to order the fluid that he needed in advance. With the help of Joe, our son, Billy, miraculously wound up performing and continuing his career for about more six years.

I could tell that the situation frustrated him. The whole sickness thing was not going away. It was steadily getting worse. Soon he had a spot on the heel of his left foot about the size of a quarter. It wasn't healing. In time, it turned black. He went to a podiatrist to see about it. His foot wasn't healing because of his diabetes.

The issue with his foot worsened. The podiatrist gave Billy exercises to help with the circulation of blood in the foot. She sent him to a nearby city for hyperbaric treatments.

That was when we found out that hyperbaric was used for more than deep-sea divers with the bends, resulting from ascending to the surface of the water too quickly. Hyperbaric oxygen therapy involved exposing the body to 100 percent oxygen at a pressure greater than what you normally experience. Wounds needed oxygen to heal properly, and exposing a wound to 100 percent oxygen can, in many cases, speed the healing process.

I even cut my vacation to Detroit short once I knew that Billy had to make a trip to Louisiana for a special foot treatment by order of his podiatrist. I wanted to help however I could. I didn't like seeing Billy out of sorts.

None of these methods worked. Billy was used to taking his health for granted, as most of us do. The exercise Billy got was singing on stage every night. I didn't do a lot of the gym myself. Billy and I loved dancing together. In fact, for a stretch of time in years past, he would do the *Rubberband Man* with me on stage; and I mean we danced like we roller-skated together, never missing a beat. It is rare to find a man that's still a dancer after you get married.

Things with The Spinners began to become more and more strained after our trip to Greece. I attributed the change to Billy's sickness getting worse, among other things. At least now I knew it wasn't other women. Billy still tried to perform, no matter what was happening to him. I admired him for him for his tenacity, but it was took its toll on their performance as a whole. The fact that The Spinners' show lineup hadn't changed in twenty odd years didn't help any. Yes, the lineup stayed with the same old songs. I began to understand why the lineup had not changed. The guys were very aware of what was happening to their partners. In spite of everything, they still performed an outstanding show. People who had seen the show years before could have easily decided to forgo another show, reasoning that they already saw the routine. Those who came in spite of that proved to be loyal fans. On top of everything else, rap was getting bigger, taking over the airwaves and commanding attention.

The tougher it got for Billy, the harder it was for me. I gained weight under the stress of it all. My blood pressure was going dangerously high. Finally, my doctor told me that if I didn't stop whatever I was doing, that I might have another stroke. This time I might not be so fortunate in my recovery, if I recovered.

Being a caregiver was becoming more complicated than I could ever have imagined. The person nearest to you that has to have the care begins to resent you. Billy turned into someone I didn't know. His foot was turning black, gangrene. Oh, the smell. I thought of all the special fragrances he used to buy from around the world. Oh well. Everything the podiatrist told him to do, he ignored. I don't know if it was because she was a woman, or because he found the whole illness was consuming his very being.

There was one person that was particularly great at being there for me. This person was Louis, Billy's brother. He would go wherever Billy was to see him, no matter the distance. Billy was in rehab around St. Augustine, Florida, which was about sixty miles from the Daytona Beach area. I drove almost every day to be with Billy. Louis and his wife, Pat, would drive the distance to visit Billy. If Billy or I needed some help, Louis was there. Billy and I went from Jacksonville to the Mayo Clinic or to wherever the doctors sent him.

Finally, I could feel Billy's exhaustion in trying to handle things. The sighs that came from him—so sad and weary. He was losing ground too quickly. I was relieved when he came home. We made trips to the podiatrist frequently. I saw the man I loved slipping away, skating backward into somewhere beyond my reach. He kept telling me how much he loved me.

His foot was getting worse. I began to smell the dying flesh. It was smell that you couldn't describe. There wasn't anything you could compare it to. I remember asking, "What is that smell?" I never smelled anything like that before. He couldn't smell it.

I knew that he had something in the back of his mind, but he wouldn't talk to me about it. These conditions were getting so bad it began to effect Billy's performance on stage. The Spinners were helpless, pursing their lips and shaking their heads as they watched him decline.

As Billy struggled, it wasn't long before Pervis, the bass singer, began to show signs of dementia. The Spinners kept the same show so that he could perform with them. His long-term memory remained fairly intact. He remembered his part, as far as singing, but didn't have the memory to be able to record new music, as far I was concerned. Special accommodations were set up with Chucky, who was their road manager at the time. He told me that he kept him from checking into the wrong hotels and such. Fred had the same testimony, as did other members of the entourage!

A low point in Billy's life come about, his relationship with the spinner ended. He finally got to the point where he couldn't perform at all, among other things. This action taken by The Spinners totally broke his heart. He could not understand it all, and neither did they. No one knew how to prepare for such sickness. Coming from the projects, all they knew was the grind of the gigs and recording.

Even with that being the case, Billy stuck his neck out for those boys. I remember Billy telling me how he saved Henry's spot in the group until he got out of the service. I witnessed his desperate call to Aretha Franklin when the group was about to break up. I remember when he paid everyone for doing a gig, and he wound up with nothing. I sat on the couch with my head in my hands, wondering how they couldn't show some deference for Billy in his time of need.

Billy sought to keep his legacy alive by getting in touch with Harvey Fuqua to form a new group. He felt that since he started the original group, he could start another group with two of his sons and some other friends.

Things got awfully lean then since Billy lost his income. He couldn't work. We had investments, savings, etc. Still we didn't know how long that would last. Harvey (who was involved with the foundation) had been instrumental in getting The Spinners nominated for the Pioneer Awards given by The Rhythm and Blues Foundation in 1997. He said that not only did the foundation give awards that were monetary, they helped distressed artists pay some of their bills. He gave us a number for me to contact. I submitted the information, and they sent me a check. This money saved us until Billy's social security came through. I was getting social security, and my check helped out as well. Billy's sister, Sally, and her husband, Johnnie, loaned us some money. Friends began to come to our aid. Thanks to everyone who helped us in our time of need!

We went from one rehabilitation facility to another close to home. Finally, the day came when he was hospitalized permanently. The kidney doctor placed him on a ventilator. I couldn't understand why. Billy was not having trouble breathing. His appetite was waning, but he still had one. We discussed the fact that we both did not want to be placed on a ventilator, if it ever came to that. We submitted a living will to the hospital signed by Billy.

I mentioned this to the head nurse attending Billy, then I spoke to the doctor, asking why Billy was being placed on a ventilator. The doctor just stared at me with a blank expression. I demanded he be taken off the machine immediately. The doctor said it couldn't be done. I spoke about suing him and the hospital for violating our written orders.

Billy was immediately taken off the machine. Right afterward, he woke up startled that he was still here. He started to eat, and his breathing was fine. Billy wanted his DVD player so that he could see some of the lectures pertaining to the Bible classes. He assumed a new attitude for recovering, and he began to fight to get better. He had been almost comatose, close to the point of no return while on the machine.

Unfortunately, Billy's change of attitude was a little late to help him. His foot became even worse. They amputated his leg up to the knee. He was placed in another rehabilitation facility. This time it was closer to home. Friends and family could visit. His sisters, Edna, Ginger, and Patty, came from out of town to see him. Not a Spinner came, not a single, solitary one.

Whatever the circumstance, he felt their allegiance would see him through. That was the biggest disappointment of all. We could barely speak of it between us, no louder than whispers. Nothing brought him back this time! He loved the guys! They forgot their oath that nothing would interfere or divide them. Nothing!

Billy was hospitalized again, now with more complications. His diabetes and his kidneys got worse. With glassy eyes and a weakened a smile, he tried hard not to let his depression show. He soon lost the other leg by amputation.

We began to talk about death upon the doctor's advice. He told us there was a very slim to none chance for Billy's recovery, that if he did, he could perhaps carry on with a prosthesis. Oh, for such a dancing man, such a joyous dancing man.

The doctor finally said that Billy was going into hospice. He explained that it was just a matter of time, and he would send someone from hospice to help us with certain decisions we would have to make. Hospice is specialized care for those facing terminal illness. It is designed to provide support for the patient and their loved ones during the final stages of the illness. Hospice focuses on comfort and quality life rather than cure. The goal of hospice care is to enable the patient to have an alert, pain-free life, to have the patient live each day as fully as possible.

With this knowledge, Billy decided to return to the same rehabilitation facility he just left. He didn't want to die at home. To some people, this might be strange. He knew that I would have to live there after he was gone and didn't want the memory of his passing to loom over the house. Even with the sickness having him out of sorts, he came back in flashes, showing unselfish love and caring.

Although in an almost numb state, I notified his family. His sister Sally and her husband, Johnny, came from out of town. They were with me every step of the way with Billy.

In a prophetic moment, Billy declared that he would stop dialysis and that, consequently, in three days, he would be dead. The following Wednesday morning, he indeed refused his dialysis treatment. I didn't know it at the time. When my girlfriend, Joyce, and I went to see him, he told us that Larry King (TV personality) was talking about him. Joyce and I looked at each other. There was no

TV in the room. We both figured he was talking that way because of the medication he was taking.

Thursday came. I went to see Billy with his sister Sally and her husband, Johnny. He was very uncomfortable, squirming slightly this and that way, but not in pain. As I tried to talk with him, I had to lean down close to him to hear his response. He kissed me. He was saying that he was tired. Again, I had to get very close so I could make out what he was saying. How I wanted to rip the sickness from his body and take him home with me!

Sally was watching. She kiddingly made a remark, "Are you guys sure you don't want me to leave the room?"

I turned around with a puzzled look, and she smiled the warmest smile. I asked Billy if he remembered saying when we got married that he would be my last husband.

Billy said in a very low weak voice, "I remember."

I told him, "You were right," and he gave me the best smile that he could.

We kissed a last time, slow, tender, innocent. I could almost feel the breeze of the skating rink on my neck. He asked me if I was going to be all right.

I answered, "Yes, I am married to *The Rubberband Man*. I have learned to snap back!"

The next morning, I received a call saying that he was gone. It was the third day, Friday. My life with him came to an end. I discovered that Larry King did indeed talk about Billy's passing.

Billy is still in my thoughts and heart. He is still my love. He was truly *The Rubberband Man*. We found the truth together. He loved me the only way he knew.

There is a course in music appreciation being taught at Daytona Beach State College all about The Spinners, which is required. Not bad for a man with an eighth-grade education!

When I hear one of their songs on the radio and in movies, such as the newly released *Avengers Infinity War*. I cover my mouth and blink back the tears. I am proud to have been a part of it all. Billy said I would never be bored. Baby, you knew your business when you said that. And with that, I am still spinning and learning.